COLLINS GEM

PREDICTING

The Diagram Group

D1380846

HarperCollins*Publishers*

HarperCollins Publishers
P. O. Box, Glasgow G4 0NB

A Diagram Book first created by Diagram Visual
Information Limited of 195 Kentish Town Road,
London NW5 8SY, England

First published 1991

Reprint 10 9 8 7 6 5 4

© Diagram Visual Information Limited 1991

ISBN 0 00 458996 3

Printed in Great Britain by
HarperCollins Manufacturing, Glasgow

Introduction

The *Collins Gem Guide to Predicting* brings together
the methods of fortune tellers from past and present,
east and west, in a fascinating way and explains how
and why these forms of divination have been
considered worthy of serious study.

More importantly, the book explains, through step-by-
step diagrams, the basic techniques of the wide variety
of methods of predicting in use today. The illustrations
and clear explanatory text – compiled by experienced
practitioners from the major fields of divination –
allow this wealth of information to be easily grasped
and put into practice at all levels, from telling fortunes
at parties to beginning serious studies in one of the
major disciplines.

Some people take predicting the future seriously;
others regard it as frivolous amusement. Whichever
approach you take, remember that even the most
sceptical can be secretly susceptible. Intuition,
discretion and sympathy are the hallmarks of good
fortune tellers, plus an awareness of their own
fallibility. Predicting the future may give us only an
indication of future trends in our lives; it is up to us
what we make of the opportunities we are offered.

Contents

Methods of predicting

Ailuromancy Reading omens involving cats. 145

Arachnomancy Reading omens involving spiders. 146

Astragalomancy Divination using two dice or astragals (sheep ankle-bones). 122

Astrology Exploring the effect of the sun, moon and eight of the planets upon the earth and its inhabitants. 180

Candles See Lychnomancy and Lithomancy.

Cards See Tarot and Cartomancy.

Cartomancy Divination using standard cards. 90

Catoptromancy Reading images in a mirror. 166

Ceromancy Interpreting symbols from melted wax dripped into cold water. 171

Clairvoyance Literally 'clear vision', analysing waking visions using extrasensory perceptions. 57

Cleidomancy Divination using a suspended key. 63

Coffee grounds An agent for divination, like tea leaves. 172

Cromniomancy Using onions for divination. 154

Crystallomancy Divination by a crystal ball. 166

Dactylomancy Divination by a suspended ring. 63

Dice An agent of divination, usually in the form of plastic cubes. 120

Dominoes An agent of divination, usually small, oblong-shaped pieces of wood or plastic. 125

Dowsing Using a stick, rod or pendulum to locate something hidden or buried. 59

Dreams See Oneiromancy.

Fingerprints See Palmistry. 51

Geomancy Interpreting patterns in the earth, usually sand, dust or soil. 159

Hippomancy Reading omens involving horses. 145

Itches An agent of divination by omens. 147

Knives/Scissors Agents of omen divination. 149

Lampadomancy Interpreting omens from oil lamps or torch flames. 149

Lamps See Lampadomancy.

Lithomancy Interpreting omens using precious stones and candles. 150

Lychnomancy Interpreting omens from flames of three wax candles. 150

Mirrors See Catoptromancy.

Molybdomancy Interpreting symbols from molten lead dripped into cold water. 171

Numerology Divination or character analysis using numbers relating to personal events or names. 131

Omens Signs from events or occurrences of coming misfortune or good luck. 141

Oneiromancy Interpretation of dreams. 53

Oriental Astrology A form of astrology (see Astrology) based on a 12-year animal cycle. 244

Palmistry Divination through studying hands. 7

Radiesthesia Divination using a pendulum. 67

Runes Agents of divination. 114

Scrying Gazing into a reflective surface. 164

Superstitions Beliefs that natural or supernatural phenomena portend future events. See omens. 141

Tarot Divination using cards in a tarot deck. 68

Tasseography Reading tea-leaves. 171

Tea See Tasseography.

Palmistry

Palmistry is a misleading name, for a great deal more than the palm of the hand is considered in this type of prediction. The experts prefer more resonantly impressive terms like 'chirognomy', 'chirology' or even 'chiromancy', from the Greek word cheir, meaning hand. But whatever you choose to call it, it remains a process rooted in the belief that you literally hold your future in your hands.

People have always been fascinated by the markings on their hands – palm prints have even been discovered in Stone Age cave paintings. Although no physical evidence exists to support their theories, some practitioners have claimed that the origins of palmistry lie far back with the ancient Egyptians, Chaldeans, Sumerians or Babylonians. It seems likely that palmistry began in the east and spread to the west, perhaps carried by the Romany peoples. The earliest verifiable references to the art seem to be in Indian literature of the Vedic period (c.2000BC) in the east, and in the works of Aristotle (384–322BC) in the west – but both these bear witness to a rich history of oral tradition on the subject. Palmistry has had a chequered history: in the 17th century it was taught at the universities of Leipzig and Halle in Germany, while at the same time it was being outlawed in England as a form of witchcraft.

Why read hands? There are thousands of nerve endings in your hands which are in direct contact with your brain, and so there is a constant two-way traffic of

impulses along the nerves. Because of this traffic, the
lines and marks on your hands are supposed to show a
reflection of your personality, to mirror your physical
and emotional condition. Palmists have always known
this intuitively: today's scientists are finding evidence
to support the theory, and some geneticists and
psychiatrists already use hand analysis to assist them in
the diagnosis of a variety of physical and mental
illnesses.

AN OVERALL VIEW

The proper place to begin both the study of palmistry
and any specific reading is with the whole hand. Or, in
fact, both hands, since your left hand is said to indicate
the potentialities that you were born with, and your
right hand to reveal your individual nature as it is now,
and what its future may be – unless you are left-
handed, when the reverse applies. The differences can
be usefully revealing of the directions the subject has
taken through life, and of the effect of the years on the
subject.

The cardinal rule in palmistry, as in all the major forms
of fortune telling, is that an overall view is essential.
You cannot hope to achieve any certain picture of your
subject's character and potential from only the shape of
the hand, or from any other isolated detail. You must
wait until all the clues have been gathered and see then
how one factor balances or compensates for another,
how different elements are reinforced, others cancelled
out and so on.

This paramount rule partly explains why good palmists
rarely make sweeping, unequivocal statements along
the lines of 'you will be rich this time next year' or

'you have only six months to live'. There are too many factors in a subject as broad and complex as palmistry. They cannot be interpreted simply, in the way of the omens of folk belief, or the flat assertions of newspaper horoscopes. What you achieve, when all the details are collated, is a probable pattern, a set of tendencies, with very little in it of fixed, unavoidable fate. Every reading, like every human being, is a mixture of good and bad.

Some further points you should remember when making your readings

First, be careful. Real hands seldom show marks as clearly as do the illustrations in this book, and you will need to have studied a great many hands before you can be completely confident in your recognition of detail. Second, be open-minded. Don't leap to conclusions about the nature of a hand, for there is then the temptation to ignore other details, or subconsciously to twist their meaning, when they do not conform to your too-hasty interpretation. Let your reading build slowly, and accept all the contradictions, divergences and inconsistencies.

Third, remember to correlate all the details into a complete, balanced picture before delivering your interpretation. Most people get along through life fairly well, with plenty of ups and downs, good times and bad, in general balancing each other out. Try to find a similar kind of balance in your readings. And finally, consider the chirognomists' assertion that destiny as revealed in the hand is not fixed and predetermined. The lines and marks can change, it is said, over a period of time, as obviously can the fleshiness of the fingers and mounts. And so good or ill omens may in fact come and go.

Map of the Hand

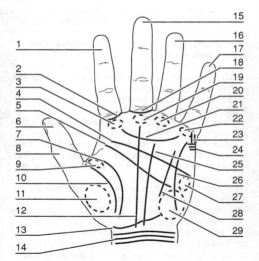

 1 Finger of Jupiter
 2 Solomon's ring
 3 Mount of Jupiter
 4 Heartline
 5 Headline
 6 Phalange of will
 7 Lifeline
 8 Phalange of logic
 9 Lower mount of Mars
10 Line of Mars
11 Mount of Venus
12 Line of Fate
13 Via Lasciva
14 Rascettes
15 Finger of Saturn
16 Finger of Apollo
17 Finger of Mercury
18 Ring of Saturn
19 Mount of Saturn
20 Mount of Apollo
21 Girdle of Venus

22 Mount of Mercury
23 Child lines
24 Line of marriage
25 Line of the sun
26 Line of intuition
27 Upper mount of Mars
28 Hepatica
29 Mount of the moon

HANDPRINTS

There is much to be said for reading a hand from a
print, rather than the hand itself. You will be in no
danger of being affected by the subject's possible
reactions to your comments as you build up the
reading. And if you keep the print safely, some years
later you can determine for yourself whether the hands
have changed in any of the details – and if so what
those changes may indicate.

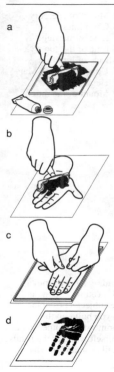

The easiest way to produce a good print is with a small roller. Squeeze out some ink (water-based for easy removal) onto a smooth surface, and pass the roller through it several times (**a**). Then use the roller to transfer a thin film of ink as evenly as possible to all the surfaces of the palm (**b**). Make the print (**c**) by pressing the subject's hand carefully but firmly onto a sheet of paper, making sure that you get a good impression of the centre of the palm as well as the fingers and thumbs – a rubber pad under the paper will be helpful. Lift the hand away carefully, making sure that you do not blur the print (**d**).

TRADITIONAL VERSUS MODERN HAND CLASSIFICATIONS

Traditionally, fortune tellers asserted that there were seven basic types of hand shape. And these seven revealed some equally traditional attitudes to society and its hierarchy – for at one end was the delicate, languid hand of the aristocrat, and at the other was the peasant's coarsened and work-hardened fist. But even so, there may be useful clues to be gained in your own readings from this old classification, and the seven types deserve to be briefly noted.

These days, however, palmists are more ready to admit that these seven rigid classifications are somewhat unrealistic. So modern palmists have refined their classification of hand shapes into only four basic types, which do tend more or less to occur in reality. They also keep a traditional flavour by relating them to the four elements of the ancient world – earth, fire, water and air – which are linked in turn with corresponding character traits.

TRADITIONAL HAND CLASSIFICATIONS

1 Elemental
A thick, broad, short-fingered hand. A slow-thinker, perhaps with a crude, physical nature.

2 Square (or useful)
A square palm, with broad and blunt fingers. A practical, conventional, unadaptable, unintellectual nature.

3 Spatulate
A spade-shaped and straight-fingered hand. An ambitious and energetic nature, independent, erratic, not much given to intellect.

4 Philosophical
Broad-palmed, with heavy joints on the fingers. A logical, cautious nature, thoughtful and introverted, analytic rather than fanciful.

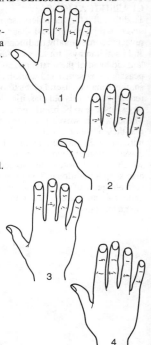

5 Artistic (or conic)
A long and flexible hand with tapering fingers. A sensitive, creative nature, more impulsive than methodical.

6 Idealistic (or psychic)
An even longer and more delicate hand. A nature far removed from harsh reality, a dreamer, mystic, aesthete.

7 Mixed
A necessary, if vague, category, since almost no-one fits precisely into just one of the foregoing six pigeonholes. Most people's hands combine two or more of the types mentioned, as do most people's natures.

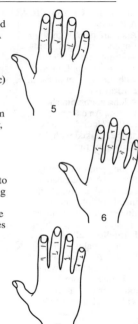

MODERN CLASSIFICATIONS

A Practical

A square palm with short fingers. An honest, hard-working, feet-on-the-ground person. Linked with the element of earth.

B Intuitive

A long palm with short fingers. An energetic, restless, individualistic nature. Linked with the element of fire.

C Sensitive

A long palm with long fingers. An imaginative, emotional nature, often moody or introverted. Linked with the element of water.

D Intellectual

A square palm with long fingers. A clever, rational, articulate nature, aware and orderly (sometimes too orderly). Linked with the element of air.

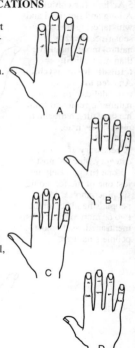

GENERAL HAND FEATURES

Whichever classification system you use, however, it will give you nothing more than a few initial hints, general pointers to start off your overall reading. Further pointers can be found in the size and texture of your subject's hand. Someone whose hand is small in comparison to the rest of their build will think and act on a large scale, behaving decisively and leaving the detail to others. Proportionately large hands indicate a thoughtful, patient mind and – surprising as it may seem – a skill with fine, delicate, detailed work.

A palm with a firm and elastic texture usually belongs to an optimistic, healthy person; a soft, flabby and fleshy palm indicates sensuality and indolence; and a hard, dry, wooden palm a tense, chronic worrier. Nearly all doctors inspect a patient's fingertips when making an examination, as the nails give important indications of a person's state of health. And just as we usually accept that people who bite their nails tend to be tense and anxious, so the shape and colour of the nails can give us hints to the character of their owner. So, as you begin your reading, carefully consider the hand as a whole before going on to look in detail at the fingers, mounts and lines. If you intend to work from a hand print, remember to take a good look at the whole hand as you make the print!

NAIL SHAPES

a Short nails Energetic, curious, intuitive, logical.

b Short nails, broader than they are long Critical and quick-tempered.

c Broad, long nails, rounded at the tip A person of clear, sound judgement.

d Long, almond-shaped nails A placid and easy-going person, a dreamer.

e Very large, square nails Cold and selfish.

f Wedge-shaped nails Over-sensitive.

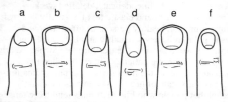

NAIL COLOUR

White Cold, conceited and selfish.

Pale pink A warm and outgoing nature.

Red A violent temper.

Bluish Unhealthy.

AREAS OF THE HAND

Palmists regard the hand as being divided into four main areas, each related to a particular facet of the personality.

A The inner active area Relating to close relationships and sexuality.

B The outer active area Relating to social attitudes and relationships with the outside world.

C The inner passive area Relating to the subconscious.
D The outer passive area Relating to energy and creative potential.

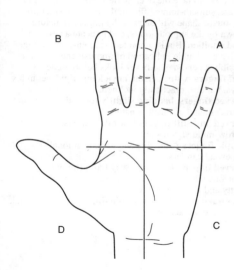

FLEXIBILITY AND BEND OF THE FINGERS

Palmists look too at the shape of the fingers, their flexibility and their position on the hand in relation to one another. They also read much into the separate segments or 'phalanges'. So, as always, you should remember to take the overall view. For example, in a square, smooth-jointed finger, the reflective qualities of the square shape will balance the impulsive nature shown by the smooth joints, and indicate a person of good intuition. But in a pointed, smooth-jointed finger we have a double indication of impulsiveness – quite possibly a person who never looks before he leaps.

Stiff fingers A stiff person, unyielding, rigid, set in his ways, but also practically inclined.

Curved fingers, bending slightly towards the palm A prudent and acquisitive nature.

Curved and stiff fingers Fearful, cautious, narrow-minded, tenacious.

Supple fingers Attractive and unconventional, somewhat careless.

Curved fingers, bending away from the palm Someone who ignores rules and regulations, who is chatty and good company.

Backward curving and supple fingers An open mind, inquisitive, attractive.

FINGER SHAPES
Long Intelligent.
Short Impulsive,
hasty, less intelligent.
Large Painstaking,
slow-thinking.
Square (1)
Thoughtful, cautious.
Spatulate (2)
Energetic.
Waisted Considerate.
Tapered (3)
Impulsive, artistic,
punctilious.
Slender Introverted,
an aesthetic nature.
Thick and short
Selfish.
Crooked Malicious,
easily irritated.
Puffy Hedonistic.
Smooth joints (4)
Quick-thinking,
impulsive.
Knotty joints (5)
Deep-thinking,
dignified.
Large joints
Methodical,
rational.

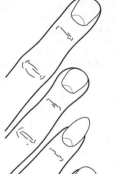

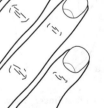

THE SET OF THE FINGERS

The second finger is never set low, but decides the level for the other fingers.

Even set (a) A person with a positive nature and plenty of common sense, one who will do well in life.

Uneven set (b) The most common set: life will be more of a battle, full of ups and downs.

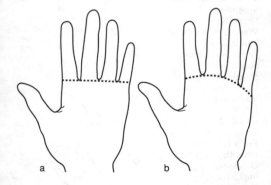

a   b

Low set first finger A shy, unassertive person who inwardly feels superior to everyone else.

Low set third finger A person frustrated in career matters, one who has had to take a job contrary to real talents and inclinations.

Low set fourth finger Nothing comes easily, and this person will have to struggle hard to succeed.

HAND SPAN

Fingers held stiffly together
Cautious, suspicious and
unsociable.

Evenly spaced fingers
A well-balanced mind, likely to
be successful in any field.

Well-separated fingers
Independent and freedom-loving.

Wide gap between all fingers
Frank, open and trusting – an
almost child-like nature.

**Widest space between thumb
and first finger** Outgoing, a
generous disposition.

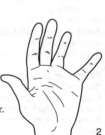

**Widest space between first and
second fingers** Not easily
influenced by others,
independent in thought and
action.

**Widest space between second
and third fingers** Free from
anxieties for the future,
light-hearted.

**Widest space between third
and fourth fingers (1)** An
independent and original thinker.

**Fourth finger very separated
from the other fingers (2)**
Difficulties in personal
relationships, isolated and
alienated.

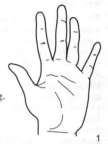

THE THUMB

For many palmists, the thumb is almost as important to
a reading as all the fingers put together. Some Hindu
palmists are known to restrict their reading to the
thumb alone, and to ignore the rest of the hand! The
thumb bears no god's name (although it is sometimes
linked with the first house of the horoscope), but it is a
key indicator of the level of vitality or life energy. The
larger the thumb, the more vital and powerful the
personality, especially when linked with a strong index
finger.

The thumb's phalanges each have their traditional
associations – the first (bearing the nail) with the will,
the second with logic. Like the fingers, the thumb
properly has three phalanges, but the third is the pad of
flesh that frames one side of the palm. This is
traditionally put together with the other similarly
prominent pads on the hand, which are known as
mounts.

Long A good leader, clear-minded, willpower
tempered by good judgement.

Very long Tyrannical, despotic, determined to get own
way.

Short Impressionable, indecisive, with the heart ruling
the head.

Large Capable and forceful.

Short and thick Obstinate.

Small and weak Lacking in energy and willpower.

Straight and stiff Reserved, loyal, reliable, cautious,
stubborn.

Flexible A flexible nature, easy-going, generous,
tolerant, tends to be extravagant.

Smooth joints Full of vitality.
Knotty joints Energy comes in erratic bursts.
High set Acquisitive, mean.
Low set (1) Courageous, versatile.
Lies close to palm (2) Not quite honest.
Bent, hidden under fingers Unhappy and self-destructive.
Forming clear right angle to palm when outstretched A strong sense of justice.
Forming an angle greater than a right angle Too tender-hearted.

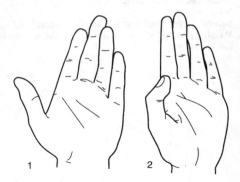

PHALANGES OF THE THUMB

Equal length (a) Well-balanced personality.

Full thumb – first and second of fairly even width (b) Blunt, outspoken.

Broad and sturdy first Plenty of stamina and well-directed energy.

First longer than second Energy uncontrolled by logic.

Very tapered first Lacks stamina and vitality.

Clubbed first (c) Violent, full of uncontrolled energy. Traditionally the 'murderer's thumb'.

Broad and sturdy second Logical, thoughtful, thinks before acting.

Second longer than first Inhibited, feels restricted.

Waisted second (d) Quick-thinking, tactful, impulsive, can be evasive.

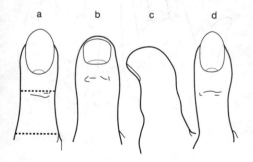

4 THE FIRST, INDEX OR FORE FINGER: JUPITER

Top level with bottom of nail on second finger
A leader, a person with the power to govern.

Top below bottom of nail on second finger Timid, feels inferior, avoids responsibility.

Same length as, or longer than, second finger (A)
A dictator, self-centred, one determined to make others obey.

Curved in a bow towards second finger Indicates acquisitiveness. This can range from collecting as a hobby if the curve is slight to hoarding and miserliness if the curve is pronounced.

Top phalange bending towards second finger
Persistent, stubborn.

Normal length, but shorter than third finger (B)
A good organiser, capable of taking charge, but preferring to work in partnership.

Same length as third finger Well-balanced and self-assured.

Longer than third finger Proud, ambitious, longing for power.

Long and smooth Good prospects in work, business and in the outside world in general.

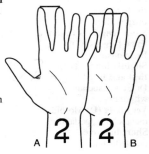

Short Lacks stamina and confidence.

Very short Self-effacing, frightened of the outside world.

Very thick Dogged and determined.

Very thin A person who will succeed in imagination but not in reality.

Crooked Unscrupulous, determined to get their own way regardless of the consequences.

Phalanges marked with deep straight vertical lines These are known as the 'tired lines'. They indicate overwork and fatigue.

♄ THE SECOND OR MIDDLE FINGER: SATURN

Straight, and in good proportion to the other fingers A prudent and sensible person, with good concentration and an ability to plan ahead, but who needs privacy.

Long, strong and heavy
Serious and thoughtful, likely to have a hard and difficult life.

Same length as first and third fingers (C) Irresponsible.

Slightly longer than first and third fingers Dry, cool, socially withdrawn.

Very long (D) Morbid, melancholic, pedantic.

Short Intuitive, unintellectual.

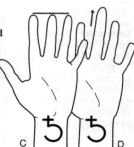

Middle phalange longest Green-fingered, loves the country.
Curved Shows the inclination to the inner or the outer side of life, depending on the direction of the curve.
Crooked Full of self-pity.

⊙ THE THIRD OR RING FINGER: APOLLO
Strong and smooth Emotionally balanced.
Smooth, with smooth joints Creative.
Long Conceited, longing for fame, wanting to be in the limelight – a good sign for those with careers in show business or advertising.
Very long Introverted.
Short (E) Shy, lacks emotional control.
Third phalange longest Desires money and luxury.
Bending towards second finger Anxiety-ridden, always on the defensive.
Second and third fingers bending together (F) Secretive.
Nail phalange bending towards second finger Afflictions of the heart – these may be emotional or physical.
Bending or drooping towards palm when hand is relaxed Has difficulty in coming to terms with the inner or intuitive aspects of the personality.

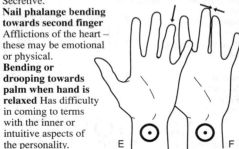

Crooked or otherwise distorted, or out of proportion to the rest of the hand Emotional difficulties.

☿ THE FOURTH OR LITTLE FINGER: MERCURY

Reaching above top crease on third finger Highly intelligent, fluent, expressive, good business ability.

Reaching nail on third finger (G) Untrustworthy.

Short (H) Difficulty in making the best of oneself.

Long first phalange Knowledgeable, considerable interest in education.

First phalange very much longer than the others Tends to exaggerate or to embroider the truth.

Short or almost non-existent third phalange Degeneracy.

Bending towards third finger Shrewd, clever in business and at making money.

Bent towards palm when hand is relaxed Sexual difficulties.

Twisted or crooked Dishonest, a liar, uses questionable business practices.

MOUNTS AROUND THE PALM

The base of the thumb, its third phalange, is called the
mount of Venus. And – like the goddess, or the planet
in astrology – this phalange brings emotional matters to
join will and logic in the thumb's overall range of
reference.

As we have already seen, the areas nearer the thumb
are concerned with our relationships with the outside
world, and those farther away with inner matters. So on
the other side of the palm is another important pad of
flesh, called the mount of the moon. And it reflects
both lunar folklore and astrological references in its
connection with intuitive, imaginative, even mystic
mental activity.

Other mounts around the palm are found at the base of
the fingers. They share the same names as the fingers
(the mount of Apollo is also known as the mount of the
sun), and usually either reinforce or counterbalance
what the fingers reveal. Worthwhile personality clues
can also come from a blurring of the boundaries
between the mounts.

Mars, the god of war, does not give his name to any of
the fingers, but instead to two mounts on the hand, the
upper and lower mounts of Mars. The upper is linked
with moral courage and resistance; the lower, roughly
triangular in shape, with physical courage and
aggression.

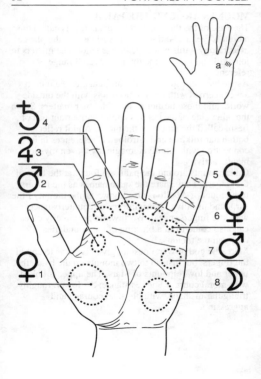

♀ MOUNT OF VENUS (1)

Broad, firm and rounded Healthy, warm-hearted, sincere, compassionate, loves children.

Flat, underdeveloped Delicate constitution, detached and self-contained nature.

Large A high degree of vitality.

Very large, overdeveloped Extremely energetic physically, hedonistic.

High and firm Highly sexed.

High and soft Excitable and fickle.

Lower part of mount more prominent Energy probably channelled into artistic concerns.

Marked with a large saltire A person who has only one great love in his life.

♂ LOWER MOUNT OF MARS (2)

Normal size Physically brave, resolute, able to keep a cool head in a crisis.

Flat, underdeveloped Cowardly, afraid of physical suffering.

Very large, overdeveloped Violent and argumentative, possibly cruel, but never afraid of taking risks.

♃ MOUNT OF JUPITER (3)

Normal size Enthusiastic, ambitious, good-tempered, friendly. Self-confident and generous. Conventional and conservative at heart, a lover of pomp and ritual.

Flat, underdeveloped Selfish, lazy, inconsiderate, lacks confidence.

Very large, overdeveloped Arrogant and overbearing, totally self-centred, driven by ambition.

Connected with the mount of Saturn Happier working in partnership than alone.

♄ MOUNT OF SATURN (4)
Normal size An introspective nature, serious-minded, studious, prudent.
Flat, underdeveloped A run-of-the-mill person with an unremarkable destiny.
Very large, overdeveloped Gloomy, withdrawn, a recluse. Possibly morbid and suicidal.
Leaning towards the mount of Jupiter A solemn person who aims high.
Leaning towards the mount of Apollo Has an intense appreciation of beauty.

☉ MOUNT OF APOLLO (MOUNT OF THE SUN) (5)
Normal size A pleasant, sunny nature, with a lucky streak. Has good taste and artistic leanings.
Flat, underdeveloped Leads a dull, aimless existence, and has no interest in the arts or any form of culture.
Very large, overdeveloped Pretentious, extravagant, and hedonistic.
Leaning towards the mount of Mercury Able to make money from the arts.
Connected with the mount of Mercury Any introvert or extrovert tendencies shown in the fingers will be reinforced.

☿ MOUNT OF MERCURY (6)
Normal size Quick-thinking but subtle. Lively, persuasive, hard-working, needs variety and company.

Flat, underdeveloped Dull, gullible, and humourless. A failure.

Large A good sense of humour.

Very large, overdeveloped A sharp conman, materialistic and light-fingered, a cheat.

Marked by short, straight lines (a) The 'medical stigmata'. Caring, compassionate, a potential healer. Usually found in the hands of doctors and nurses.

♂ UPPER MOUNT OF MARS (7)

Normal size Morally courageous.

Flat, underdeveloped Cowardly, interested only in self-preservation.

Very large, overdeveloped Bad-tempered, sarcastic, mentally cruel.

☽ MOUNT OF THE MOON (8)

Normal size Sensitive and perceptive, romantic and imaginative, artistic, possibly with a great love of the sea.

Flat, underdeveloped Unimaginative, unsympathetic, unstable, cold, bigoted.

Very large, overdeveloped Over-imaginative, introspective, probably untruthful.

High and firm Creative, with a powerful and fertile imagination.

High and soft A touchy, thin-skinned, fickle dreamer.

Reaching to the mount of Venus Extremely passionate.

Reaching towards the wrist Indicates the possession of occult powers.

MAJOR AND MINOR LINES

The three major lines – the head, heart, and life lines –
appear on nearly every hand. Although it is possible to
have one or more of these lines missing, in practice it is
unlikely that you will ever see such a palm.

The lifeline does not indicate how long you will live:
the old wives' tale that a short lifeline indicates a short
life should be forgotten. What the lifeline does show is
the strength of a person's vitality, their 'life energy',
and so it should be read in conjunction with the thumb,
the finger of Jupiter and the mount of Venus, which are
also important in this area. Similarly, the heartline,
which is concerned with our emotions, should be
referred to those other indicators of our feelings, the
finger of Mercury and the mount of Venus.

The headline is concerned with our mental attitudes.
Like all the lines in the palm, it should be related to the
shape of the hand. For example, you would normally
expect to find a straight headline on a practical hand: a
sloping headline would be unusual. (It could indicate a
person who uses their imagination in a practical way,
perhaps a designer or inventor.) But a sloping headline
on a sensitive hand would merely act as a confirmation
of the imaginative nature you had already suspected.

Unlike the major lines, the minor lines – the line of
fate, the line of the sun, and so on – can be present or
absent. Indeed, the lines on the palm can and do
change, growing clearer or less clear, developing
disruptions or losing them. So it would not be
surprising to see a strong line of fate (the most
changeable of all the lines) in the hand of an adult
where there had not been one in the child. And in some

cases, we would certainly prefer the line to be absent:
the more robust your constitution, the less likely you
are to have the misnamed line of health in your hand.
Of the more commonly occurring lines, the line of fate
relates to our destiny; the line of the sun to our good
fortune, and to our creativity; the girdle of Venus to
passion; the Via Lasciva to our desires – for money,
sensual pleasure and so on; and the bracelets to health,
wealth and travel. The lines of health, marriage,
children and influence have their own eponymous
spheres of influence.

HEADLINE

Length This indicates the level of intelligence,
breadth of understanding and use made of intellectual
potential. The longer the line, the greater the
importance played by intellectual matters.

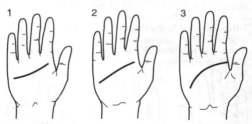

Straight across palm (1) Practical and realistic, down-
to-earth, a good organiser.
Long and straight Shrewd, a good forward planner
with a good memory.

Sloping towards mount of the moon (2) Sensitive and imaginative.

Long, reaching top part of mount of the moon (3) A talent for self-expression.

Long, reaching lower part of mount of the moon Over-imaginative.

Running towards centre of wrist Out of touch with reality.

Curving up towards heartline Good business ability, good at making money.

Running close to heartline Narrow in outlook.

Weak and some distance from lifeline A tendency to gamble.

Clear and distinct Good concentration.

Chain-like appearance Poor concentration, scatterbrained.

Break in the line A traumatic event with a far-reaching effect on mental attitudes.

Discontinuities in the line Changes in mental attitudes, but less traumatic.

Starts just touching lifeline (4) A prudent, moderate and balanced nature.

4

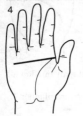

5

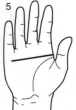

6

Starts with a small separation from lifeline (5)
Independent and enterprising, in need of a definite
direction in life to prevent wasting energy on trivia.
Starts with a wide separation from lifeline (6)
Foolhardy and excitable.
Starts linked to lifeline for some distance (7)
Very cautious. Needs encouragement, responds badly
to criticism.
Starts inside lifeline on mount of Mars (8) Touchy,
irritable.

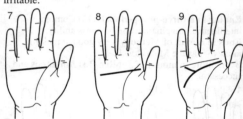

**Ends with a large fork that touches both the mount
of the moon and the heartline (9)** Able to be
subsumed in another's personality, will give up
everything for love.
Long, sloping, ends with a fork Clever and
diplomatic, with a talent for self-expression.
**Straight, ends with a small fork pointing to the
mount of the moon (10)** Imagination restrained by
common sense.
Ends in a large fork (11) Too versatile, unable to
achieve excellence in any one thing.

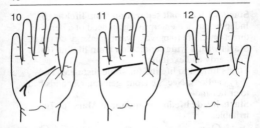

Ending in a three-pronged fork (12) Combines intelligence, imagination and business ability.
Ends in mount of Mercury Very good at making money – has the Midas touch.
Branchline to mount of Jupiter (13) Ambitious and successful.

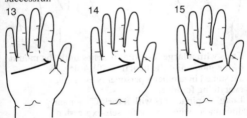

Branchline to mount of Saturn (14) Ambitious, but will have to struggle for success.
Branchline to mount of Apollo (15) Achieving success through the use of own talents.

Branchline ending between third and fourth fingers
A successful scientist or inventor.

Branchline to mount of Mercury Successful in business.

HEARTLINE

Long, generously curved and some distance from the bases of the fingers Warm-hearted, sensual, demonstrative.

Longer and stronger than headline The heart rules the head.

Straight Reserved and self-interested.

Short and faint A limited capacity for love.

Very long, deep and close to the fingers Possessive, jealous.

Chain-like appearance A flirt.

Blurred appearance Tendency to emotional difficulties.

Many small branches (l) A vivid, dynamic personality. Each branch represents a romantic attachment, pointing upward for those that are successful and downward for those that are not.

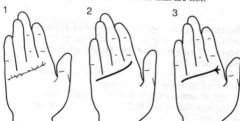

Broken in several places Unfaithful, lacks constancy.
Broken under second finger Jilted.
Broken under third finger A jilt.
Broken sections overlapping A temporary separation.
Starts in middle of mount of Jupiter (2) Fussy and discriminating when choosing friends and lovers, extremely loyal to those chosen. Seeks to marry well.
Starts with a fork on mount of Jupiter (3) Lovable and easy to live with, makes a good marriage partner.
Starts with a large fork, one prong on mount of Jupiter and one on mount of Saturn (4) Changeable, moody, has difficulty in living with others.

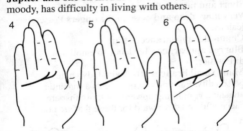

Starts between fingers of Saturn and Jupiter A relationship that involves friendship as well as love.
Starts on mount of Saturn (5) Sensual, but lacking real depth of feeling for others.
Chain-like appearance and starting on mount of Saturn Contempt for the opposite sex.
Starts at same point as headline and lifeline Extremely selfish and lacks any control over the emotions.

Branchline running to headline (6) A partner met through work, or a marriage that is a working partnership.
Running together with headline as one line Known as the 'simian line'. A sign of enormous internal struggle, possibly of mental handicap.
Branchline running to fateline A romance, if the branchline does not touch the fateline; a wedding if they just touch; an unhappy marriage if they cross.

LIFELINE

Long and clear Good vitality, a healthy constitution.
Short and chequered Lacks energy, may be physically frail.
Chain-like appearance Alternating enthusiasm and torpor, energy coming uneasily in fits and starts.
Discontinuities in the line Changes in the direction of life.
Break in the line on one hand only An illness, followed by a speedy recovery.
Break in the line on both hands A more serious illness.
Many small branches running upward Good health, prosperity.
Many small branches running downward Poor health, financial setbacks.
Starts on mount of Jupiter (7) Highly ambitious – and likely to succeed.
Starts from headline (8) Very controlled and calculating.
Starts well below headline (9) Lacks control, uninhibited.
Ends in a fork with one branch ending in mount of the moon Indicates long-distance travel.
Branchline to mount of Jupiter Self-confident and self-assured.

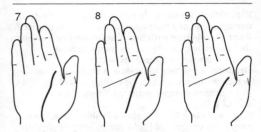

Two small branches from beginning of line onto headline (10) An inheritance: could be money, but more likely to have been given a good start in life by parents.

Branchline to headline from halfway down line (11) Success and recognition will come in middle age.

Branchline to mount of Saturn Life will be a struggle, must make own way without outside help.

Branchline to mount of the sun (12) Talents will be recognised and rewarded.

Branchline to mount of the moon A longing for a new stimulus, for change. Traditionally, a sea journey.

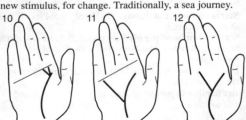

LINE OF FATE

No line A smooth and uneventful life.
Straight and unbroken A successful, untroubled life.
Chain-like sections Indicate unhappy periods in life.
Wavy Argumentative, changeable, disorganised.
Break in the line Sudden change in circumstances.
Broken sections overlapping Planned major changes.
Short bar across line Setback or obstacle.
Reaching mount of Saturn Trying to exceed own powers.
Curved towards mount of Jupiter Success through effort.
Starts from headline or heartline Success late in life.
Starts from lifeline (13) Hampered by early environment and family surroundings. Point of separation of lines shows when independence was or will be achieved.
Starts from top bracelet (14) Early responsibility.
Starts from mount of the moon A varied life, much travelling.
Starts from mount of Venus, ends on mount of Saturn (15) A secure and loved childhood, supported by parents and family. Possibly success through inheritance.

13   14   15

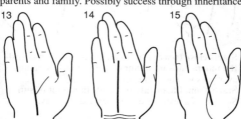

Ends on headline Prone to errors of judgement, bad planning that leads to misfortune.

Ends on heartline Sacrifices necessary in the cause of love or duty.

Ends on mount of the sun Popular and talented.

Branchline to line of the sun A successful partnership. If the lines cross, the partnership will fail.

Branchline to mount of Mercury Achievement and wealth obtained through business or science.

LINE OF THE SUN (LINE OF APOLLO)

No line A life of disappointments and setbacks, however talented the owner of the hand.

Clear and straight A lucky person with a charming and sunny nature.

Blurred Lacks concentration, wastes effort.

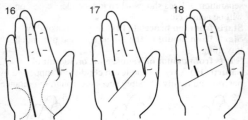

Starts close to wrist between mounts of Venus and the moon, ends in mount of the sun (16) Nothing ever goes wrong in this life.

Starts from life or fateline, ends in mount of sun Success as a result of using talents and energy.

Starts from headline (17) Success in middle age as result of own efforts.
Starts from heartline (18) Warmth, happiness, and sufficiency in old age.

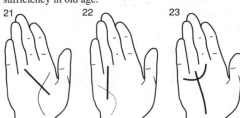

Starts from mount of Venus (19) Artistically gifted.
Starts from mount of the moon (20) Strongly attractive to the opposite sex, a person idolised by the masses.
Ends in many small lines Unsettled, with many conflicting interests.
Ends in a fork with prongs on mounts of Mercury, Saturn and Apollo (21) Lasting success on a firm base.

1 GIRDLE OF VENUS
No line A well-controlled, calm personality.
Well-marked Over-emotional, craves excitement and variety.
Short Keenly aware of the feelings of others.
Blurred or broken Over-sensitive.
Crosses lines of fate and the sun Witty, talented.

Ends on mount of Mercury Enormous reserves of energy, but a tendency to go to extremes.

Runs off side of the hand instead of making a semicircle Vacillating, a ditherer.

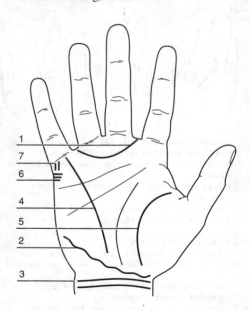

2 VIA LASCIVA (MILKY WAY)

Straight Restless, easily bored.

Straight and long, reaching mount of Mercury An eloquent speaker of dubious morality.

Curved A person who is his own worst enemy.

Curved, and beginning inside mount of Venus Liable to take things to excess. Someone who could easily become addicted – to drugs, alcohol etc.

Branchline reaching to line of the sun Potential riches if the lines do not quite touch. Financial losses as the result of a relationship (e.g. an expensive divorce settlement) if they cross.

3 RASCETTES (BRACELETS)

Parallel and clearly marked A healthy, wealthy, long and peaceful life.

Chain-like top bracelet Eventual happiness after a difficult life.

Top bracelet arching into the palm in a woman's hand Possible difficulties in childbirth.

Line from top bracelet to mount of Jupiter A long and profitable journey.

Line from top bracelet to mount of the sun A trip to a hot country.

Line from top bracelet to mount of Mercury Sudden wealth.

Lines from top bracelet to mount of the moon Each line represents a journey.

4 HEPATICA (LINE OF HEALTH)

No line A strong and healthy constitution.

Deeply engraved Low physical resistance.

Wavy Digestive problems.

Blurred Lack of physical stamina.

Touches lifeline Take extra care of health at that time.

5 LINE OF MARS (THE INNER LIFELINE)

When present Sustains life in time of illness or danger.

6 LINES OF MARRIAGE

Strongly marked A marriage or close relationship. The number of lines indicates the number of such relationships.

Weakly marked Each line indicates a minor romantic attachment of little importance.

Long and straight A long and happy relationship.

Broken A divorce or separation.

Broken lines overlapping A reunion after a separation, perhaps remarriage to the same person.

Double line A relationship with two people at the same time, the relative depths of the relationships being indicated by the strength of the lines.

Curves downward Will outlive partner.

Strong curve upward to base of little finger Staying unmarried but not celibate.

Curve upward to line of the sun A marriage to a famous or wealthy person if the lines do not quite touch. If the lines cross, the marriage will be unhappy.

Starts with a fork Delay or frustration at the start of a relationship.

Ends in a fork A separation of some kind.

Crossed by a line running from base of finger of Mercury Opposition to a relationship.

Crossed by girdle of Venus An unhappy marriage, a nagging partner.

7 CHILD LINES

When present The lines run from the base of the finger of Mercury to the marriage lines. The number of lines are said to indicate the number of children, with the stronger lines representing boys, and the fainter lines girls.

FINGERPRINTS

Fingerprint patterns are established about 18 weeks after conception. Unlike the other lines on the hand, from then on they are fixed and unchanging. This, as we know, makes them very useful in the detection of criminals, but they can also be useful in the detection of personality. When more than one type of fingerprint pattern appears in a hand, their different characteristics will be blended in the personality. The number of fingers involved can give us an indication of the balance of that blend: a person with several fingers showing tented arches is likely to be considerably more stubborn than a person with just one!

Palmists also literally read between the lines. The area between the lines of head and heart should be a neat and well-defined oblong for the best possible portent of a balanced and steady progress through life – and nearly smooth, empty of all the collections of tiny lines found elsewhere. Otherwise there may be a tendency to imbalance, extremism of one kind or another and a somewhat erratic and fitful life. And the larger the triangular area formed by the lines of head, life and health, the better the omen.

A Low arch Hard-hearted, insensitive, sceptical, unemotional and materialistic.

B Tented arch Highly strung, artistic and impulsive – but stubborn.

C Loop Mild-tempered and straightforward, with a quick, lively and versatile mind.

D Whorl An individualist with a strong, definite personality. Potentially brilliant, best when self-employed.

E Mixed A mixed-up and muddle-headed personality. If you have any difficulty in differentiating one type of pattern from another, look for the triadus (**F**). An arch print does not have a triadus, a loop print has one and a whorl has two.

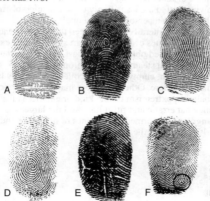

Oneiromancy

Everyone dreams, but not all dreams foretell the future.
Long before Freud and other psychoanalysts showed us
just how many of our dreams come from our
subconscious and unconscious minds, Aristotle had
argued that precognitive dreams were impossible. But
history is full of well-attested precognitive dreams
(Abraham Lincoln's dream of his own assassination is
perhaps the most famous), and so their existence
cannot be dismissed out of hand.

Oneiromancy – divination by dreams – is known
everywhere in the world. No-one knows when it began,
but records of prophetic dreams and their
interpretations survive from the most ancient cultures.
The oldest surviving comprehensive book of dreams
and their meanings was compiled by Artemidorus of
Ephesus in the 2nd century: it was translated into
English in the 17th century, reprinted 32 times before
1800, used by Freud in his researches and still
influences the dream dictionaries available today.

DREAM INTERPRETATION

The more clearly you remember a dream, the greater is
said to be its significance. But dream images fade
rapidly from the conscious memory; keeping a pencil
and paper beside your bed and writing down your
dreams as soon as you wake up will prevent you
forgetting any important details.

If you think a dream may be precognitive, break it
down into its separate elements and consider them
individually. Ignore any that relate to your everyday

life: for example, if you commute to work by train each morning, a train appearing in your dream will have no significance. Ask yourself if any events in your recent past or in your earlier life or childhood could have caused a particular image: if so, ignore that element of your dream as well.

Use a dream dictionary to interpret the elements of your dream that remain. Begin with the most important – the image that you recall most vividly – but include all the details, however minor or contradictory, in your final overall interpretation.

Which dreams?

Precognitive dreams usually occur between 3.00 am and 7.00 am, when digestion has been completed and the mind and the body are both relaxed. Dreams that do not foretell the future and have no prophetic value include those:

a occurring during the early part of the night;

b caused by indigestion or illness;

c with a reasonable outside cause – noise, temperature, sleeping position etc.

d caused by a disturbing book, television programme etc.

e concerning the events of the previous day.

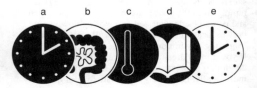

Dream images classified

(a) Any sharp-edged object – e.g. knife, scissors, sword etc. – tells of bad news to come.

(b) Clean, shiny objects are omens of good fortune; dirty, dull objects are omens of ill fortune.

(c) Ascending in any way – e.g. up ladders, stairs, ropes, escalators etc. – is always a sign of success. Descending or falling indicates reverses or failures. The higher you ascend, the greater your success; the farther you fall, the greater the setbacks.

(d) Dreams of being entertained can indicate either good or ill fortune. If you dreamed that you enjoyed a radio or television programme, a movie or a play at a theatre, the omens are good; if you were bored, or the performance was cancelled, or you disliked what you saw, the omens are bad.

(e) Depending on their appearance and/or their contents, some images can indicate either a favourable or an unfavourable future. For example, a full cupboard indicates plenty, an empty cupboard want. Similarly, calm water indicates good fortune, rough water difficulties, and murky water ill luck. Other images with comparable variations of interpretation include the following:

air	cellar	grass	plants
bank	clouds	hamper	roads
barn	cup	harvest	sky
bowl	drink	landscape	smells
bridge	farm	letters	straw
broom	field	market	vine
cage	garden	pantry	warehouse
canal	glass	paths	wind

(f) Obstacles in dreams indicate the severity of the difficulties facing you. For example, a door that opens easily suggests minor difficulties, while one that will not open at all suggests insurmountable obstacles. Other obstacles in dreams include the following:

abyss	embankment	island	struggling
barefoot	envelope	jumping	tower
bolts	examinations	labyrinth	traffic
canyon	fence	locks	valley
cave	floods	mountain	walking
cavern	gate	prison	wall
cliffs	gravel	questions	window
crutches	hedge	rivalry	zipper
ditch	hills	rocks	
drawer	hunting	sewing	

(g) Some dreams are considered to be 'dreams of contrary', i.e. their meaning is the opposite of the image. For example, a dream of misery and crying is considered an omen of happiness. Other dreams of contrary include the following:

ambition/setbacks	inferiority/superiority
calm/disturbance	losses/gains
criticism/appreciation	luxury/poverty
encouragement/discouragement	quarrels/affection
fear/courage	rejoicing/regrets

Clairvoyance

Clairvoyants have no need of the apparatus and
symbolism required by other fortune tellers: their
foreknowledge comes in the form of waking visions that
can be actively and consciously summoned when they
are wanted.

Shamans, soothsayers, witch doctors, seers, oracles and
prophets throughout the world have always relied on
their clairvoyant talents. And while many of history's
most famous clairvoyants are now more or less legendary
figures (like Cassandra, who was given the gift of sight
by Apollo, who also ordained that her prophecies should
never be believed), there are still a great many people
alive today whose foreseeings have often proved
startlingly accurate. The best-known modern clairvoyant
is probably the American Jeane Dixon, who claims to
have predicted the assassination of President Kennedy.
Although she has quite a high failure rate, she has been
correct in her predictions often enough to take her
statistically beyond the level of mere chance.

Developing clairvoyance

It is generally assumed that either you have the gift of
clairvoyance or you do not. Some people seem to have
clairvoyant powers instantly at their command, while the
rest of us seem to have no insight into the future at all.
But many authorities now believe that clairvoyant ability
is a widespread human potential. They place it in the
same mental area as intuition, and suggest that everyone
has it to some extent, even if it is latent and lying
undiscovered. They remind us of the many well-attested

cases of ordinary people with no previous history of
psychic ability who have had precognitive experiences
at moments of unusual stress.

Many clairvoyants assert that these latent abilities can
be activated. They suggest deep forms of meditation to
relax the mind, to shed the restrictions of rationalist
and materialist thinking and to put you in touch with
the deeper levels of your psyche. Some suggest that if
your rational inhibitions are very strong a course of
hypnosis may be beneficial, because it can sometimes
be the entrance into a semi-trance state that clears away
the barriers that are repressing the intuitive, paranormal
mental areas. They also recommend that you use any
form of device or tool that you find useful to
concentrate these non-rational mental areas, and to
activate and focus the extrasensory gifts.

EXTRASENSORY PERCEPTIONS

Clairaudience Literally, 'clear hearing'. Divination by
hearing the future.

Clairvoyance Literally, 'clear seeing'. Divination by
seeing the future.

Metagnomy Divination by sights of future events seen
when in a hypnotic trance.

Precognition Inner paranormal knowledge of the
future.

Psychometry Clairvoyant divination about a specific
person through holding an object belonging to him.

Dowsing

Most people think of dowsing as a technique used for
finding water in arid areas. But it can be used to find
almost anything under the earth: to locate mineral
deposits (metals, coal, oil etc.); to trace underground
pipes, tunnels and cables; to hidden treasure, lost
property and archaeological sites; and even to discover
dead bodies.

Dowsing would appear to date back to at least 6000BC–
a cave painting of that period found in the northern
Sahara shows a man holding a forked stick just as a
modern diviner would do. Certainly dowsers appear in
early Egyptian, Chinese and Peruvian carvings. From
the 15th to the 17th century, dowsers searched mainly
for metal, and were often attached to the staff of
prospecting and mining expeditions. In the 18th and
19th centuries, they usually looked for water. And
today's dowsers are often employed by public
corporations or in industry to pinpoint unmapped
cables, pipelines and so on.

In the past it was probably in the professional dowser's
own best interests to let people believe that his gift was
extremely rare. But today's experts think it is much
more likely that over 80% of us have the ability lying
latent, and could – with practice – become competent
dowsers. The equipment needed is minimal: you can
choose between the traditional forked twig or the more
sensitive divining rods. At first the reactions you obtain
may be weak, but they should become stronger with
practice. With experience, it should be possible to tell

from the strength and nature of the reaction exactly
what you have found and how deep it is buried.

DOWSING EQUIPMENT
Making metal divining rods

Cut through a wire coat hanger in two places as shown
(1), and then bend the smooth piece of wire to a right
angle (2). Repeat with a second coat hanger. The rods
can be held in the hand as they are (3), or you can
make secondary sleeves that slide over the rods and
allow them to move freely (4). A very good sleeve can
be made by removing the refill and stopper from an old
ballpoint pen.

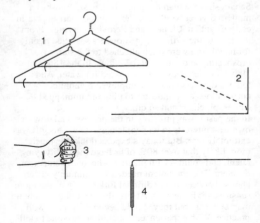

Choosing a dowsing twig

Choose a supple, pliable twig of young (but not green) wood. Hazel is the most popular, but beech, apple, birch, willow and privet can all be used. Do not choose a brittle wood that breaks easily.

Look for an undamaged, Y-shaped twig, with a strong joint at the Y. It should be about 3/8in (1cm) in diameter, and as even as possible. Cut it from the branch as shown (**5**). Use a sharp knife to trim the twig, but leave the bark on (**6**).

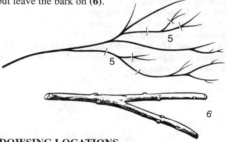

DOWSING LOCATIONS
Dowsing outdoors

If you are using metal divining rods, hold them in your loosely clenched fists, with your thumbs resting over your forefingers. Your forearms and the arms of the rods should be horizontal and parallel to each other, and your elbows should be well tucked in (**A**).

If you are using a dowsing twig, hold it firmly with your palms pointing upward and your thumbs pointing outward. The twig and your forearms should be in the same horizontal plane, and your elbows should again be well tucked in (**B**). Move your fists apart until the twig is tensed but balanced.

Concentrate your mind on the substance you are looking for: some dowsers find it helpful to carry a sample with them. The sample should be small enough to carry comfortably, but large enough to be in contact with both your skin and the rod (liquids can be carried in a small bottle). A sample is not usually needed when searching for water, as its influence is so powerful. Walk slowly and steadily over your search area, taking fairly short strides. Cover the area methodically, and use markers to indicate the places where your rods or twigs reacted. The rods will react by crossing (**C**) or by swinging apart; the twig may turn up (**D**) or down, or even revolve completely.

Dowsing indoors

Instead of working outdoors on the site, some dowsers prefer to remain indoors and to search for their sources by running their rods over a large-scale map of the area. For this type of work many dowsers prefer a more accurate pointer in the form of a pendulum. Using a pendulum for divination is known as radiesthesia. The earliest form of radiesthesia seems to have been coscinomancy, or divination by sieve. The suspended sieve was held in the air in a pair of tongs, which were kept closed by two people's fingertips. The sieve was then said to answer questions or to indicate the name of a guilty person by the way in which it rotated. Other forms of the art included divination with a suspended key (cleidomancy) or a suspended ring (dactylomancy) – methods that are still in use today.

Some radiesthesists practice forms of medical divination. The pendulum is held over various parts of the afflicted person's body, and the radiesthesist reads in its movements the location and diagnosis of the ailment. The pendulum is even said to be able to predict the onset of illness, and so to advise in preventive medicine. And it can apparently work without the presence of the patient: the medical radiesthesist may hold the pendulum over a sample of blood or urine, or perhaps merely over a photograph of the sufferer. But probably the commonest use of radiesthesia on the human body is in attempting to detect the sex of an unborn child.

Choosing a pendulum

Many dowsers prefer their pendulums to be made of natural materials, especially wood; an average size pendulum would be about 1-2in (2-5cm) in diameter, and 1-2in (2-5cm) long. A cavity pendulum (**1**) can be used to hold a sample of any specific substance you are searching for.

But pendulums can be made in any material, and in any size and shape. You can choose from those commercially available (**2**, **3**, **4**, **5**), or you could use a

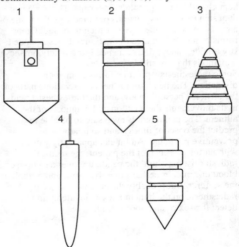

pendant or medallion (6), a large needle on a thread (7), a key tied to a piece of thin string (8), or a carved crystal on a gold chain (9). A woman who wishes to discover the sex of her unborn child traditionally uses a pendulum made from her wedding ring suspended on a hair from her head (10).

As long as the pendulum can swing freely and easily, the string or cord can be of any length from a few inches to about 2ft (60cm); a typical length is 5-6in (12-15cm).

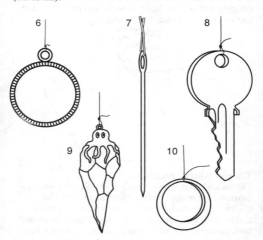

Using the pendulum

The pendulum should normally be held in your
dominant hand. Hold the cord between your thumb and
forefinger, allowing them to form a circle, and spread
out your other fingers so that they are facing down. The
arm should be firmly braced, but without tension.
Cover your search area methodically, working very
slowly across the map or photograph and marking any
reactions you obtain.

The pendulum can also be used outdoors instead of a
divining rod or twig, but it is very susceptible to wind
and so can only be used on a calm day.

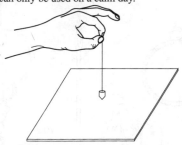

The pendulum's reactions

The pendulum is unusual in divination in that its
movements are apparently sex-related (one of its
traditional uses is in detecting the sex of an unborn
child). With most operators, the pendulum will swing
backward and forward (**A**) to indicate a man or a boy
and around in a circle (**B**) to indicate a girl or a woman.

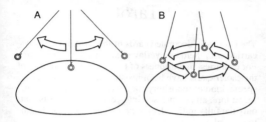

But with other operators these actions may be reversed – just as some people are right-handed and others left-handed.

Sex-determined movements apart, the pendulum's reactions seem to be particular to every individual dowser or radiesthesist. It is worth looking for known substances at first so that you can assess just how your pendulum reacts – it may oscillate a different number of times or in a different direction for different substances, or you may need to lengthen or shorten the cord to get a clear reaction. And although not everyone has the full range of radiesthesic talents, you may find that you are able to use your pendulum to answer specific questions (getting one reaction for 'yes' and another for 'no'), to act like a compass in directing you or to tell you the time. By recording all the details of the gyrations of your pendulum under known conditions, you will be able to prepare your personal calibration chart for future reference.

Tarot

The exotically decorated cards of the tarot have always carried with them an overlay of slightly sinister mystery. For centuries, practitioners of the occult and students of the esoteric arts have been insisting that the tarot is a special kind of repository for a vast amount of ancient, secret lore, all compressed into codes and symbols that only the fully initiated, and the very learned, can begin to unravel.

Origin

Part of this mysterious reputation comes from the fact that no-one can be sure where or when the tarot first came into existence. The puzzle of its origin has led some occultists to claim that it goes all the way back to the sorcery-steeped priests of ancient Egypt, ancient Babylon or ancient Tibet – or even, some have said, ancient and lost Atlantis. But other people have been in no doubt about the tarot's inspiration, if not its origin, when they have labelled it 'the devil's picturebook'. Devils and mysteries aside, what is certain about the tarot is that it made its first recorded appearance in medieval France, in about 1390. And it is possible that the cards evolved as part of the secret folklore of the Romany peoples (gypsies) and came to Europe with them during their westward migrations centuries ago. Nor did it stop evolving, even after its use spread beyond the Romanies. The ordinary deck of cards that we use today for bridge or poker grew out of the tarot, and many modern occultists have redesigned the tarot cards, omitting some and changing the basic nature of others, to create more up-to-date or more personalised sets. But the traditional tarot of Europe, which became more or less fixed and standardised by the 18th century, remains the most impressively decorative, and the most richly furnished with shadowy symbolism.

It is not difficult to acquire tarot cards. If the place where you live does not have a shop that specialises in such esoteric merchandise, you can probably get them by mail order through an advertisement in one of the more popular occult or fortune-telling magazines. It is considerably more difficult, however, to acquire the ability to use the tarot. Each card has, of course, its own essential 'meaning', its basic area of symbolic reference, explained on the following pages. But knowing those basics is like knowing how to move the pieces on a chess board: you can participate, but there is much more to know before you can become accomplished.

Tarot and intuition

Many different styles of tarot cards are available. Choose a deck that you respond to intuitively.

Each one of the tarot cards brings with it a long, dark train of symbolism, of subtle hints and echoes, references and connections, which resonate far into the depths of the occult tradition, and should also resonate into the intuition of the skilled fortune teller. So you are advised, by the experts, to take the tarot seriously – to go on in your reading beyond the basics, and to become familiar with those resonances. You are also advised to handle your own tarot cards as much as you can, to study the cards, think about them, attune them to your own intuitive awareness. And you are advised to treat them with respect. The tarot, it is said, will not be mocked. If you approach it light-heartedly, using it to answer frivolous questions and the like, the tradition says that you may receive answers you would rather not have had.

But if all this sounds a little ominous, it should be added that in medieval times people used tarot cards to play quite ordinary, and presumably frivolous, card games – often for money. And history does not record that they suffered any ill effects.

Tarot cards: an overview

In any case, whether you intend to devote your life to mastering the tarot, or merely wish to add it to your collection of techniques for occasional fortune telling, you must start at the same place – with an overall look at the cards themselves.

There are 78 tarot cards, of which 56 divide into the sequential cards of the four suits. The suits are cups, swords, pentacles and wands, which respectively are the ancestors of our modern hearts, spades, diamonds and clubs. (The ancestry is even more obvious in modern European card decks: hearts in Spain are *copas*, cups; spades in France are *piques*, pikes; and so on.) Obviously there must be 14 cards in each suit: the intruder is an extra court card, called the knight, which was not retained in the modern deck.

The 56 cards of the four suits are known as the minor arcana (from 'arcane' – secret), and they have their special meanings and symbolisms, and their own uses in fortune telling. But the main concern of the fortune teller is with the remaining 22 cards, the major arcana, sometimes known as the greater trumps. And with them we enter a positive labyrinth of rich, dark and resonant symbolism.

THE MAJOR ARCANA

The 22 greater trumps form the secret heart of the tarot.
The most decorated of the 78 cards, the most densely
packed with occult significance, they will serve on their
own, without the other cards, for enough varieties of
fortune-telling practice to keep you busy for years.
Especially when, as the specialists would warn, you
could spend those years merely finding your way
through the labyrinth of mystic symbolism, before ever
beginning to deal them out for a reading.

But, because not everyone has the time or inclination to
become a fully fledged occultist, these pages are
offered as a simplified, preliminary map through the
main routes of that labyrinth, so that – without too
much effort – you can begin fairly promptly to make
some use of the major arcana.

Traditionally the 22 cards are numbered and named (or
at least 21 of them are numbered, as will be seen).
Because scholarly experts like to disagree with one
another, there has always been some argument about
their proper order, and their true names. But we can cut
through the argument by democratically following the
majority view over the centuries. In the same way the
meanings of each of the 22 cards that are given here, in
capsule form, are attempts at synthesising the most
widely accepted areas of symbolic reference attached to
each card.

Meanings

Aside from their individual meanings, the cards are said to fall into some neat groupings that can offer useful guidelines to the fortune teller. Most important, all 22 of them can be seen to represent stages in the individual's progress through life, from the Fool (i.e. the innocent newborn) through to the 'completion' symbol of the World, with the Wheel of Fortune at midpoint. The first 11, the first half of life, tend to be outward-looking, oriented towards the world of positive action and development. The second 11 bring the individual to a more inward-looking time, meditative and quiet, focused on inner development. Tarot cards are of course not double-headed, and so will sometimes be laid upside down during a reading. Most experts have believed that being reversed in this way alters their meaning. Some modern fortune tellers, however, have chosen to discount this extra complication, but to dismiss a substantial part of the tradition in that way seems a trifle high-handed. So the following capsule definitions of the major arcana include abbreviated notes on the reversed meanings – which are often just the direct opposite of the card's essential implications, but can sometimes carry more subtle overtones.

Cards of the major arcana

Alternative names used in different decks are given in brackets.

0 (or unnumbered) Fool
1 Magician (Juggler)
2 High Priestess (Juno, Papess, Female Pope)
3 Empress
4 Emperor
5 High Priest (Jupiter, Pope, Heirophant)
6 Lovers
7 Chariot
8 Justice
9 Hermit
10 Wheel of Fortune
11 Strength
12 Hanged Man
13 Death
14 Temperance
15 Devil
16 Tower (Falling Tower)
17 Star
18 Moon
19 Sun
20 Judgement (The Last Judgement)
21 World
(In some sets, card 8 is Strength
and card 11 is Justice.)

O The Fool

Unnumbered, and has been placed at number 22. The most complex and most human of the cards – 'holy innocent', wise man and trickster, with all of humanity's contradictions (male/female, good/evil, angel/devil etc.). Symbol of potentiality, new beginnings, fresh challenges. Often used as the significator, to represent the person who is the subject of a reading.
Reversed Beware of foolish lack of forethought.

1 Magician

Only a step away from the Fool (as jester) and so relating more to a stage magician, an entertainer, than to a master of high magical lore. A fortunate card, suggesting progress in outward, worldly understanding, and progress also towards success. Its appearance suggests decisions to be made, with confidence.
Reversed Warns against hesitation, or against an unwillingness to confront the real world.

2 High Priestess

Injects an element of intuition, special knowledge, creativity, the non-rational, natural side of wisdom and understanding (including the psychic sort). Indicates a female influence, and the prospect of light being shed on a secret or problem.

Reversed Warns against over-emotionalism, irrationality, insufficient use of rational thought.

3 Empress

Expresses the fertility principle, the bountiful, caring, loving, enriching symbol of the Earth Mother. Another fortunate card, indicating a solid stability and also a natural growth and creativity (perhaps a new baby, material prosperity or just general well-being).

Reversed Domestic trouble and insecurity – perhaps sexual difficulties or career setbacks.

4 Emperor

Male symbol who is the father figure to the Empress's mother. Indicates worldly success, authority and power, the triumph of rationality, outward energy and strength of will. A fortunate card for men; for women, it can mean a dominating male influence, or achievement of ambition through forcefulness and controlled aggression.
Reversed Warns against weakness, submission.

5 High Priest

Spiritual rather than worldly power and authority – and the male counterpart of the High Priestess, offering rational knowledge, wisdom, creative intelligence, inspiring perceptions. Indicates the gaining of insight and understanding, not necessarily religious, always profound yet sensible. Can refer to the influence of an important teacher or adviser.
Reversed Beware of lies, misleading advice.

6 Lovers

Has to do with love relationships, obviously, and contains all the conflicts – choices to be made between the attractions of the flesh and of the spirit. A card that suggests a rewarding relationship or a good marriage, and extends to indicate generally positive decisions.
Reversed A wrong choice will be made, perhaps involving sexual infidelity. Also warns of sexual difficulties.

7 Chariot

Symbol of movement, indicating travel and, more generally, progress and achievement. (Some of this is also contained within the 'lucky' number of the card.) Signifies an important stage has been reached in the outward advance through worldly life, with obstacles overcome and success gained through personal dynamism.
Reversed Beware of too much dynamism leading to ruthlessness.

8 Justice

A useful balance to the preceding success card, the Chariot. A reminder of the need for balance and sound judgement, awareness that a complete person needs more than material triumphs – that heart and spirit must also be served. The card also means that the person is to be judged – which can be positive unless the subject is found wanting.
Reversed Injustice, harsh or unfair judgement by others.

9 Hermit

Like Justice, a card that shows the tarot moving away from outward advance towards less-worldly and less-material considerations. Suggests a need for revaluation, inner growth and development, perhaps for counsel about the future.
Reversed Warns against imprudence and stubbornness, a refusal to stop and think things out or to take wise advice.

10 Wheel of Fortune

Another clear sign of a new stage or beginning. Change must come, or life will stagnate, and luck will play a part in decisions to be made. A fortunate card, implying that destiny will work itself out positively. Alludes to the mystic idea of karma, individual inner growth toward wholeness and harmony (symbolised by the circular mandala).

Reversed Ill luck, decline, adversity, changes for the worse.

11 Strength

Indicates the need to face new developments with courage, fortitude, moral fibre. Implies setbacks and difficulties, yet the card is fortunate, for it suggests that inner resources will overcome these adversities. (Some experts prefer to transpose the positions of this card and Justice, but our ordering is as valid.)

Reversed Obstacles will not be overcome, due to lack of moral or spiritual strength.

12 Hanged Man

When this card is right side up, the figure is upside down. Implies risk or sacrifice, perhaps a decision to abandon worldly values, and to plunge into the depths of the self, to seek the inner reality needed to become whole. From that sacrifice comes enlightenment and renewal.
Reversed Beware a rigid refusal to accept that there is more to life than the practical, rational world.

13 Death

Not at all ominous, despite the name, number and image. It takes the preceding card a step farther: for true inner development, a kind of death of the worldly self is required, so that an inner, spiritual, psychic rebirth can be achieved. Also implies that every setback or failure can bring new understanding, and therefore new hope.
Reversed Foreshadows destruction without renewal.

14 Temperance

Another of the tarot's virtuous abstractions, emphasising the need for moderation, and reminding us that a truly complete life exhibits a harmony between the material and spiritual sides of things. In short, don't go too far 'inward'. A fortunate card for all enterprises demanding the balancing of many complex factors.
Reversed Difficulty and setbacks caused by lack of harmony.

15 Devil

A distinctly ominous card, reflecting what can happen if we let some of our 'inward' qualities – such as sexual impulses, selfishness, the urge to wield power – get out of control or out of balance. Yet, controlled, the strength of those drives can be positive, an energy source for more admirable development.
Reversed Warns against giving way to base impulses, the dark side of our nature.

16 Tower

Another unfortunate card, a clear picture of ruin and destruction, of hopes and ambitions being shattered. But there is a positive side: out of destruction can come rebuilding, out of suffering can come understanding – once the lessons are learned and the painfully acquired perceptions have been assimilated.
Reversed Ruin and calamity needlessly brought upon oneself.

17 Star

A fortunate card, also indicating the hope of renewal after calamity. It promises new and rich horizons, perhaps in previously unforeseen directions – once one has been tempered and enlarged by having come through the bad times. A card of enlightenment and enhanced awareness.
Reversed Warns against spiritual blindness that prevents seeing or taking advantage of new horizons.

18 Moon

All the irrational, supernatural associations of the moon can make this an unfortunate card for the rational person, because it indicates a time when only intuition, the non-rational side, can overcome obstacles. Yet the non-rational must be used with care, for it can lead toward a dangerous fantasy world.
Reversed Warns against fearing the non-rational and settling for a life of stagnation and sterility.

19 Sun

Beyond the moonlit passage of darkness, a burst of sunlit success and happiness. The goal is visible: illumination in every sense, adversity overcome, wholeness and harmony achieved (another circular mandala). The card signifies the triumphant reward for coming through hardships.
Reversed Failure, the collapse of hopes, or at best a superficial, dubious success.

20 Judgement

Not to be confused with Justice, this card concerns a day of judgement – when you pause to weigh up what you have done, and what you have become, in your passage through life. A fortunate card, indicating that you have achieved worthy goals, have attained inner development, and are now entering a time of serenity and happiness, a time of new beginnings.

Reversed Regrets, remorse, recriminations.

21 World

The final stage, the ultimate circular mandala symbolising completion, triumph, fulfilment. And because the major arcana can be seen as a circle, a closed cyclical system, you can see it moving on to the Fool again, beginning a new cycle but perhaps on a higher plane, with greater goals.

Reversed Ultimate failure rather than ultimate fulfilment, a bleak immobility, the inability to progress on and up.

THE MINOR ARCANA

As the name minor arcana indicates, the remaining 56
tarot cards have far less range and richness of meaning
for fortune telling. So you may feel inclined to leave
this section aside for a while, until you feel more at
home with the mysteries and meanings of the 22 great
cards that have just been described.

But a time may come when you want to expand your
fortune-telling horizons and aspire to the use of the
whole tarot. So the following pages provide capsule
introductions to the spheres of influence where the
minor arcana has relevance.

Once again, if the card is dealt upside down, its
meaning is reversed – but usually in an even more
explicitly opposing or extreme manner than with the
major arcana. So these fairly obvious reversed
meanings have not been included here.

In a reading using the lesser cards, you can choose a
significator – a card that represents the person who is
the subject of the reading – from among the court
cards. It should usually correspond with the subject in
sex, complexion and (where possible) personality.

Choosing the significator

For a reading for a fair-haired young woman, use the
queen of cups.

For a fair, mature woman (especially if well-to-do), use
the queen of pentacles.

For a dark and perhaps dangerous woman, use the
queen of wands.

For a dark and sad woman, use the queen of swords.

For a fair young man, or any young man in love,
use the knight of cups.

For a wealthy young man, use the knight of pentacles.
For a dark young man, use the knight of wands.
For a dangerous young man, use the knave of wands.
For a fair-haired mature man, use the king of cups.
For a wealthy mature man, use the king of pentacles.
For a mature man in a position of power, use the king of swords.
For a dark and/or dangerous mature man, use the king of wands.

TAROT SUITS
Spheres of influence
Each tarot suit has its own symbolic sphere of influence and relevance. Cups (**a**) relate to emotional matters, love, sex, marriage, fertility and creativity. Pentacles (**b**) have to do with wealth, finance, commerce, prosperity and economic security. Swords (**c**) concern activity and progress, opposition and conflict, the need to impose order on chaos. Wands (**d**) relate to the mind, the world of ideas and deep thought, intellectual strength, range and purposefulness.

a   b   c   d

SUIT OF CUPS
Ace of cups Fertility, love, abundance.
Two of cups Love, friendship, harmonious connections.
Three of cups Happiness and joy from love.
Four of cups Emotional joy (but beware of excess).
Five of cups Joy turned sour, loss, reassessment.
Six of cups Happy memories, the past reawakened.
Seven of cups Ambition, hope (with forethought).
Eight of cups Disappointment, search for new paths.
Nine of cups Peace, contentment, fulfilment.
Ten of cups Peace again, happiness, achievement.
Knave of cups A thoughtful, helpful youth.
Knight of cups A bright, cheery youth, a lover.
Queen of cups A fair, loving, creative woman.
King of cups An intelligent, successful, worldly man.

SUIT OF SWORDS
Ace of swords Success, attainment of goals.
Two of swords Good fortune out of adversity.
Three of swords Benefits from paths being cleared.
Four of swords Serenity, calm, respite from struggle.
Five of swords Further struggle, possible defeat.
Six of swords Difficulties surmounted, travel, good news.
Seven of swords Difficulties – be brave and careful.
Eight of swords Difficulties – be patient.
Nine of swords Disaster and failure – be steadfast.
Ten of swords Disaster, the darkest hour before dawn.
Knave of swords A clever, even guileful young man.
Knight of swords A soldier, a dark, strong youth.
Queen of swords A dark, clever woman, a widow.
King of swords A dark, authoritative man.

SUIT OF PENTACLES
Ace of pentacles Material prosperity.
Two of pentacles Disruptions in material matters.
Three of pentacles Achievement in business.
Four of pentacles Wealth, pinnacles of success.
Five of pentacles Ruin, financial collapse.
Six of pentacles Financial aid, stability.
Seven of pentacles Material progress, but be wary.
Eight of pentacles Rewards for care and effort.
Nine of pentacles Riches, achievement.
Ten of pentacles Wealth, an inheritance.
Knave of pentacles A careful, sensible youth.
Knight of pentacles A good, honourable young man.
Queen of pentacles A sensible, generous, wealthy woman
King of pentacles A careful, practical, successful man.
SUIT OF WANDS
Ace of wands Inspiration and new beginnings.
Two of wands Good fortune, well deserved.
Three of wands Gains from brave initiatives.
Four of wands Success and popularity.
Five of wands Setbacks and obstacles – be determined.
Six of wands Achievement, encouraging news.
Seven of wands Troubles, but promising prospects.
Eight of wands Forward progress – be confident.
Nine of wands Opposition – be unyielding.
Ten of wands Obstacles and struggles.
Knave of wands A dark, lively youth, an employee.
Knight of wands A dark, energetic man, a journey.
Queen of wands A practical, dominant woman.
King of wands A powerful, determined man.

Cartomancy

As modern playing cards evolved from the tarot deck, it is not surprising that they are used to predict the future. The 52 cards in a standard deck are derived from the tarot's minor arcana; four court cards – the knights – have been dropped. The only trace remaining of the 22 cards of the major arcana of the tarot is the Fool, who has become the joker of the modern deck. The current standard deck in use around the world is of French origin, probably introduced in the late 15th century. Cards were then painted by hand or printed with woodblocks; they were not mass manufactured until 1832. They were originally made to be viewed from one direction only (as tarot cards still are) – the double-headed playing card was not introduced until the late 19th century.

The interpretations of the individual cards in predicting the future probably also derive from the tarot. Until comparatively recently, the interpretations were preserved only in the oral tradition, and so can vary from source to source, or perhaps appear confusing or contradictory. The interpretations given here are those that are most generally accepted today.

Divination using playing cards

You can use the full deck of 52 playing cards when you are trying to read the future – or, if you prefer, you can discard all the twos, threes, fours, fives and sixes, and use only the remaining 32-card deck. Both decks will give you equally good results. Use whichever you prefer, but make sure not to confuse the two: the meanings of the individual cards in the 52-card deck are not the same as those in the 32-card deck, and the methods of laying out the cards also vary. But the areas of influence of the four suits do not change whichever deck is used, nor does the choice of client card or your general preparation before laying out the cards.

The influence of the suits

When you are laying out the cards for a reading, you may find that one suit is more strongly represented than the others. As each suit is said to have its own particular area of influence, you must take this into account in your reading, and allow the atmosphere conveyed by the prominent suit to modify your interpretation of the other cards.

Hearts are considered lucky. Your emotions and your domestic life – love, affection, friendship, marriage, the family – are all said to be under their influence. They also stand for ambitions successfully realised.

Clubs are the cards of success and are connected with money, business and loyalty. But they can also be associated with failure, betrayal and financial worries.

Diamonds influence your life outside your home. They also suggest that ambitions can only be realised and money made through hard work.

Spades warn of dangers ahead. Your misfortunes – loss, suffering, enemies, treachery, failure – are all said to be under their influence.

Client card

The 'client card' is a king or queen selected to
represent the person who is the subject of the reading.
As far as possible, choose a card that corresponds with
your subject's age, sex and hair colour.

For a fair-, grey- or auburn-haired older man, use the
king of diamonds.

For a fair-, grey- or auburn-haired older woman, use
the queen of diamonds.

For a fair- or auburn-haired younger man, use the king
of hearts.

For a fair- or auburn-haired younger woman, use the
queen of hearts.

For a dark-haired older man, use the king of spades.

For a dark-haired older woman, use the queen of
spades.

For a dark-haired younger man, use the king of clubs.

For a dark-haired younger woman, use the queen of
clubs.

Preparing to read the cards

Choose the client card for your subject, and place it in
the centre of the table. Ask your subject to shuffle the
cards thoroughly, and then cut them with the left hand;
you should both concentrate fully on the cards, clearing
your minds of all other thoughts. Arrange the cards
around the client card in your chosen layout, and begin
the reading.

You may wish to have a general indication of your
subject's fortunes before you begin a complete reading.
After shuffling, your subject should cut the deck into
three with the left hand. Read the bottom cards of each
of these three small decks, first separately, and then in

combination. These cards will show whether the reading to come will be propitious – or otherwise. Ask your subject to shuffle and cut the cards again before you lay them out for the full reading.

It is traditionally considered unlucky to read your own future in the cards, or to read the cards when you are alone. It is also said that you should not read the cards for a particular subject more than once a week, or the cards will lose their power. But each complete reading may include repeated deals of the cards, providing that these extra deals are only used to clarify confusing indications in the original layout.

TAROT SUITS AND MODERN SUITS

The traditional symbols used on playing cards in different countries of the world are all derived from the symbols of the four suits of the tarot, as shown in the table on the following page.

Cards from the tarot's suit of wands and its derivatives are illustrated.

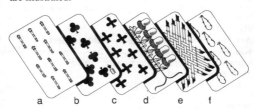

a   b   c   d   e   f

Deck	Suits			
Tarot	cups	wands (a)*	pentacles**	swords
English	hearts	clubs (b)	diamonds	spades
French	hearts	trefoils (c)	squares	pikes
German	hearts	acorns (d)	bells	leaves
Italian	cups	rods (e)	money	swords
Spanish	cups	sticks (f)	gold	swords

* Also known as the suit of batons
**Also known as the suit of coins

DIVINATION WITH THE 52-CARD DECK

When you use a full deck of 52 cards for divination,
you need make no attempt to establish whether a card
is upright or reversed: its meaning will be the same in
both cases.

HEARTS

Ace The home. Love, friendship and happiness.
King A good-natured, impetuous, fair-haired man.
Queen A trustworthy, affectionate, fair-haired woman.
Jack A close friend.
Ten Good fortune and happiness.
Nine 'The wish card' that makes dreams come true.
Wealth, status and good luck.
Eight Invitations and festivities.
Seven False hopes and broken promises, an unreliable
person.

Six An overgenerous disposition, unexpected good fortune.

Five Jealousy, indecisiveness.

Four Changes, delays and postponements (especially of marriages).

Three Warns of a need for caution.

Two Success and prosperity.

CLUBS

Ace Wealth, health, love and happiness.

King An honest, generous, dark-haired man.

Queen An attractive, self-confident, dark-haired woman.

Jack A reliable friend.

Ten Unexpected money, good luck.

Nine Friends being stubborn.

Eight Opposition, disappointment, the taking of reckless chances.

Seven Prosperity – providing a member of the opposite sex does not interfere.

Six Business success.

Five A new friend or a successful marriage.

Four Fortunes changing for the worse.

Three Marriage bringing money. May indicate several marriages.

Two Opposition and disappointments.

DIAMONDS

Ace Money, a letter or a ring.

King A stubborn, quick-tempered, fair-haired man.

Queen A flirtatious, sophisticated, fair-haired woman.

Jack A relative, not altogether reliable.

Ten Marriage or money, a journey, changes.

Nine Restlessness. A surprise connected with money.

Eight A marriage late in life. A journey leading to a new relationship.
Seven Heavy losses.
Six A warning against a second marriage.
Five Prosperity, good news, a happy family.
Four An inheritance, changes, troubles.
Three Legal or domestic disputes.
Two A serious love affair.

SPADES

Ace Emotional conflict, an unfortunate love affair. Sometimes regarded as the 'death card'.
King An ambitious dark-haired man.
Queen An unscrupulous dark-haired woman.
Jack A well-meaning but lazy acquaintance.
Ten Misfortune and worry.
Nine Bad luck in all things.
Eight Trouble and disappointment ahead.
Seven Sorrow, loss of friendship.
Six Some improvement in circumstances.
Five Reverses and anxieties, but eventual success.
Four Jealousy, illness, business worries.
Three Faithlessness and partings.
Two Separation, scandal, deceit.

SPECIAL COMBINATIONS: USING 52 CARDS

Some combinations of cards have special meanings when the deck of 52 cards is used. These meanings apply only when the cards are immediately next to one another in the layout.

Ace of hearts next to any other heart Friendship.
Ace of hearts with another heart on each side Love affair.
Ace of hearts with a diamond on each side Money.

Ace of hearts with a spade on each side Quarrels.
Ace of diamonds/eight of clubs A business proposal.
Ace of spades/king of clubs A politician.
Ace of spades/ten of spades A serious undertaking.
Ace of spades/four of hearts A new baby.
Ten of hearts Cancels adjacent cards of ill fortune; reinforces adjacent cards of good fortune.
Ten of diamonds/two of hearts Marriage bringing money.
Ten of spades Cancels adjacent cards of good fortune; reinforces adjacent cards of ill fortune.
Ten of spades next to any club Business troubles.
Ten of spades with a club on each side Theft, forgery, grave business losses.
Nine of hearts next to any card of ill fortune Quarrels, temporary obstacles.
Nine of hearts/five of spades Loss of status.
Nine of clubs/eight of hearts Gaiety.
Nine of diamonds next to any court card Lack of success, an inability to concentrate.
Nine of diamonds/eight of spades A bitter quarrel.
Nine of spades/seven of diamonds Loss of money.
Eight of hearts/eight of diamonds A trousseau.
Eight of hearts/five of hearts A present of jewellery.
Eight of diamonds/five of hearts A present of money.
Eight of spades on the immediate right of the client card Abandon your current plans.
Four of hearts next to any court card Many love affairs.
Four of clubs next to any court card A loss, injustice.
Two of clubs/two of diamonds An unexpected message.

EXAMPLES OF READINGS USING 52 CARDS

Seven triplets

This spread, also known as the seven packs, is used to give a general picture of the client's future. Use the full 52-card deck, and place the client card face up in the middle of the table. After shuffling, deal the first 21 cards face down in the order shown by the numbers on the diagram. Beginning on the left, turn up each pack of three cards and interpret them.

The client is a dark-haired young woman; her client card is the queen of clubs (**C**).

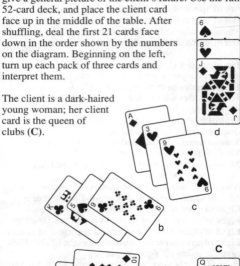

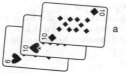

Positions on the seven triplets spread

Pack **a** Personality and state of mind.
Pack **b** Family and home.
Pack **c** Present desires.
Pack **d** Hopes and expectations.
Pack **e** The unexpected.
Pack **f** The immediate future.
Pack **g** The more distant future.

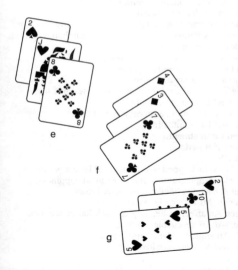

DIVINATION WITH THE 32-CARD DECK

The 32-card deck is formed by discarding the twos, threes, fours, fives and sixes from a standard 52-card deck. You will need to mark the top of each card in a 32-card deck: the meanings of the individual cards differ depending on whether they are upright or reversed.

HEARTS

Ace Good news, love, domestic happiness.
Reversed A move, changes, short-lived happiness.
King An affectionate, generous, fair-haired man.
Reversed A deceitful person.
Queen An affectionate, dependable, fair-haired woman.
Reversed A widow, divorcee, or woman unhappy in love.
Jack A friend or lover.
Reversed An untrustworthy lover.
Ten Good fortune and happiness.
Reversed A surprise, a birth.
Nine The 'wish' card that makes dreams come true.
Reversed Temporary troubles.
Eight An invitation, a journey, a wedding.
Reversed Unrequited love.
Seven Contentment.
Reversed Boredom.

CLUBS

Ace Good luck, good news, financial letters or papers.
Reversed Unpleasant letters, short-lived happiness.
King A friendly, honest, dark-haired man.
Reversed Minor worries and troubles.
Queen An affectionate, helpful, dark-haired woman.
Reversed An unreliable woman.
Jack An amusing, dark-haired lover.
Reversed An insincere lover.

Ten Luck, luxury, prosperity.
Reversed Business troubles, a journey.

Nine Unexpected money.
Reversed A small gift, or a slight problem.

Eight Joy and good fortune, brought by a dark-haired person.
Reversed An unhappy love affair, a legal dispute, a divorce.

Seven Minor money matters.
Reversed Financial problems.

DIAMONDS

Ace A letter, money or a ring.
Reversed Bad news.

King A powerful fair-haired or gray-haired man.
Reversed Treachery, deception.

Queen A spiteful, talkative, fair-haired woman.
Reversed Malice.

Jack A messenger, employee or person in uniform.
Reversed A trouble-maker.

Ten Moving house, a journey, a major change.
Reversed Changes for the worse.

Nine News, surprises, anxieties.
Reversed Domestic disputes, lovers' quarrels.

Eight A love affair, a short journey.
Reversed A separation, affections ignored.

Seven Teasing, criticism, a small gift.
Reversed Minor scandal, gossip.

SPADES

Ace Emotional satisfaction, business propositions.
Reversed Bad news, disappointments, death.

King An untrustworthy dark-haired man, possibly a lawyer.

Reversed An enemy.

Queen An older dark-haired woman, probably a widow or a divorcee.

Reversed A cunning, treacherous woman.

Jack An ill-mannered young person, possibly connected with medicine or law.

Reversed A traitor.

Ten Grief, a long journey, confinement.

Reversed Minor illness.

Nine Loss, failure, misfortune.

Reversed Unhappiness for a close friend.

Eight Bad news, impending disappointments.

Reversed Quarrels, sorrow, separation, divorce.

Seven New resolutions, a change of plan.

Reversed Bad advice, faulty planning.

SPECIAL COMBINATIONS: USING 32 CARDS

Some combinations of cards have special meanings when the deck of 32 cards is used. These meanings apply only when the cards are immediately next to one another in the layout.

Ace of clubs with a diamond on each side Money coming.

Ace of clubs/nine of diamonds Legal affairs.

Ace of diamonds/eight of clubs Unexpected money.

Ace of diamonds with a diamond on each side Financial prosperity.

Ace of diamonds/seven of diamonds Quarrels.

Ace of diamonds/seven of diamonds/jack of diamonds A cable or telegram.

Ace of diamonds/nine of spades Illness.

Ace of spades/queen of clubs A tiresome journey.

Ace of spades/nine of spades Business failure.

Ace of spades/eight of spades Betrayal.

King of hearts/nine of hearts A happy love affair.

King of clubs/ten of clubs A proposal of marriage.

King of diamonds/eight of spades An unexpected journey.

King of spades/seven of clubs Be cautious with your investments.

Queen of hearts/seven of diamonds Unexpected delights.

Queen of hearts/ten of spades Danger, adventure.

Queen of clubs/seven of diamonds An uncertain future.

Queen of diamonds/seven of hearts Happiness tainted by jealousy.

Queen of diamonds/seven of spades Success in the village rather than in the city.

Queen of spades/jack of spades Great evil.

Jack of hearts/seven of clubs A lover motivated by greed.

Jack of clubs/jack of spades Business difficulties, financial losses.

Jack of diamonds/nine of spades Beware of bad advice.

Ten of hearts/nine of clubs Show business.

Ten of hearts/ten of diamonds A wedding.

Ten of clubs next to any ace Large sums of money.

Ten of diamonds/eight of clubs A honeymoon.

Ten of diamonds/seven of spades A delay.

Ten of spades/seven of clubs An unfortunate future.

Nine of hearts/nine of clubs A fortunate legacy.

Nine of clubs/eight of hearts Celebrations, festivities.

Nine of diamonds/eight of hearts Long-distance travel.

Eight of hearts/eight of diamonds New and important work.

Eight of clubs/eight of diamonds True love.
Eight of diamonds next to any club A prolonged journey.
Eight of spades/seven of diamonds Help needed.
Seven of diamonds next to any club Money problems.
Seven of spades/king, queen or jack of spades A traitor.

QUARTETS, TRIPLETS AND PAIRS

It is considered to be very significant when two, three or four cards of the same value are immediately next to one another in the layout. These groups should be interpreted first, as they have an influence on the layout as a whole.

Four aces Separation from friends or from money. The more aces reversed, the greater the separation.

Three aces Flirtations, foolishness and temporary anxieties. The more aces reversed, the greater the folly and anxiety.

Two aces A marriage. Two red aces – a happy marriage; a red ace and a black ace – an unhappy marriage; one ace reversed – potential marriage breakdown; both aces reversed – divorce.

Four kings Good fortune, which lessens with each king reversed.

Three kings A new venture. The more kings reversed, the less successful it will be.

Two kings A business partnership. One king reversed – partially successful partnership; both kings reversed – partnership will fail.

Four queens A party or some other social gathering. The more queens reversed, the less successful it will be.

Three queens Visitors and conversation. The more queens reversed, the greater the degree of scandal and gossip attached to the visit.

Two queens Friendship. One queen reversed – rivalry;

both queens reversed – betrayal.

Four jacks Quarrels. The more jacks reversed, the more violent the quarrel.

Three jacks Family disagreements. The more jacks reversed, the greater the disagreement.

Two jacks Loss or theft, with each jack reversed bringing it nearer.

Four tens Unexpected good fortune, which lessens with each ten reversed.

Three tens Financial and legal problems, which lessen with each ten reversed.

Two tens Changes at work bringing good fortune. Each ten reversed delays them.

Four nines A pleasant surprise. The more nines reversed, the sooner it will happen.

Three nines Health, wealth and happiness. The more nines reversed, the longer they will be delayed.

Two nines Small financial gains. Each nine reversed delays and lessens the gain.

Four eights Success and failure mixed. The more eights reversed, the higher the proportion of failure.

Three eights Love and marriage. The more eights reversed, the less the degree of commitment.

Two eights A brief love affair. One eight reversed – a flirtation; both eights reversed – a misunderstanding.

Four sevens Enemies, mischief-makers. The more sevens reversed, the less successful they will be.

Three sevens A new enterprise, or a new baby. Each seven reversed delays it.

Two sevens A new and happy love affair. One seven reversed – deceived in love; both sevens reversed – regrets in love.

EXAMPLES OF READINGS USING 32 CARDS
The fan
This spread is used to give a general reading of the
client's future. Shuffle the 32-card deck and spread it
out face down on a table. Ask your client to choose any
18 cards and to set them out face up in the order
shown. If the client card is not among cards 1-13, look
for the seven of the same suit, which is an acceptable
substitute; if neither card is there,
the reading should be left
to another day.
Cards 1-13 are read
first. Considering
the client card
as the first
card, count
five cards to
the right
and interpret
the fifth card.

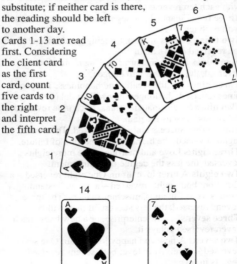

Use that card as the first card of the next set of five, and continue reading every fifth card until you have returned to the client card. Then read cards 14-18: interpret cards 14 and 18 together, then cards 15 and 17, and finally card 16. Summarise all your interpretations into a coherent reading.

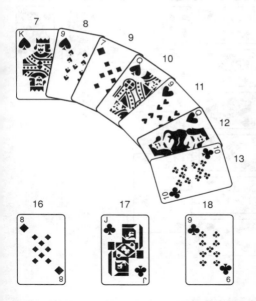

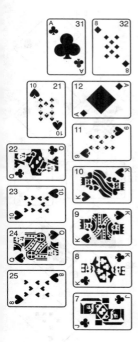

The temple of fortune

This spread dates from the middle of the 18th century, when it was developed by a famous French cartomancer called Etteilla. It gives a complete reading of the client's life – past, present, and future.

The 32-card deck is used; a client card is not required. After shuffling, the cards are laid out face up in the order shown. Cards 1-6 and 13-16 represent the past; cards 17-21 and 26-32 represent the present; cards 7-12 and 22-25 represent the future. In each case the outer row of cards gives the primary indications of the reading, which are then modified by the inner row. Some cartomancers also consider that the outer rows refer to events in the client's outer, worldly life, while the inner rows refer to the inner, mental, and spiritual life.

Grand star

The popular star spreads are found in a number of traditional forms. Of these, the grand star is probably the most useful for a general reading. The 32-card deck is used. Place the client card (**C**) face up in the centre, and deal the first 21 cards of the shuffled deck face down around it in the order shown. Turn up and interpret the cards in pairs, in the order **13**, **15**; **20**, **18**; **14**, **16**; **19**, **17**; **9**, **5**; **11**, **8**; **10**, **6**; **12**, **7**; **3**, **1**; **4**, **2**. Read the final card, **21**, on its own. Cards above the client card represent success and achievements to come; those below refer to the past, and to things already accomplished. Cards to the left of the client card represent obstacles and opposition; those to the right refer to the future, and to help and assistance to come.

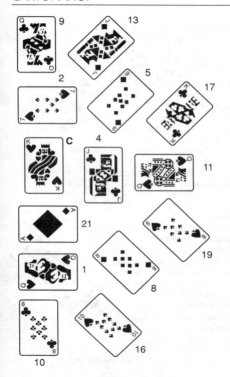

Great Star

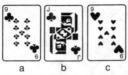

a   b   c

This is the most detailed of the
traditional star spreads. The 32-card
deck is used, and the client card
(**C**) is chosen and placed face up on
the table. The client then shuffles the deck
and divides it into three.

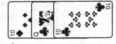

Turn each of these piles
face up and read the
three cards exposed,
first singly and then
in combination. These cards
(**a, b, c**) are called the indicators and give
the general tone of the reading. Remove
them from the deck and place them to
the left of the table. Reshuffle the
deck and deal the star in the order
shown. Interpret each group of
three cards in conjunction,
beginning with the group
immediately above the client
card and continuing in a
counterclockwise direction.
Finally, study the spread as a
whole and summarise your interpretation.

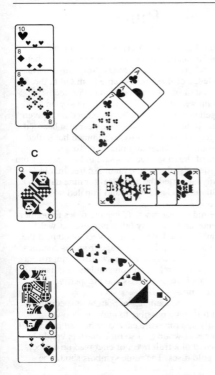

C

Runes

In about the 1st or 2nd century AD the Germanic
peoples of Northern Europe began using an alphabet
made up of characters called runes. Norse myth says
that knowledge of these runes came from Odin, the
one-eyed god of occult wisdom and the protector of
heroes. Odin was said to ride through the sky on an
eight-legged horse, and to be accompanied by a raven
and a wolf. To humans, he would appear as a bearded
man in a grey cloak, with a wide-brimmed hat pulled
forward to shade his piercing blue eye. To gain
knowledge of the runes, Odin is said to have hung from
the world-tree Yggdrasil (the giant ash tree that in
Norse myth supported the universe) for nine days and
nights, without food and water and impaled on his own
spear.

The Norse rune masters would use the runes to predict
future events, and for many other purposes as well.
Runes would be used to heal, to protect, to control the
weather or to help a prisoner escape from his enemies.
They would also be engraved on swords to improve a
warrior's fighting ability, and on amulets or talismans
worn to attract love, happiness and prosperity.

Making the runes

Sets of runes can sometimes be bought in specialist
shops, but it is quite possible to make your own.
Traditionally, the runes are carved or burned into small
oblong pieces of wood (Norse rune masters would have
used the wood of a fruit tree), or engraved on copper,
bronze or gold discs. The runic symbols should be

inscribed on one side only; the other side remains
blank. Alternatively, you can make rune cards by
drawing the runes on small squares of white board.

Reading the runes

Clear your mind of thoughts, and scatter the runes face
down in front of you. Ask the enquirer to shuffle the
runes (as if they were dominoes) and then to arrange 13
of them in a circle, still face down. The layout of this
circle – called the runic wheel – and the order in which
the runes should be set out are shown in the diagram.
Turn the runes in the wheel face up and begin your
interpretation. Each rune should be related to the rune
on either side of it, to the rune immediately opposite it
and to the centre rune. Runes are in their upright
position if their tops face the centre of the wheel; the
tops of reversed runes face the outside of the wheel.
Each position on the runic wheel is also connected with
a different aspect of life: these are listed on the next
page and should be taken into account in your reading.

Positions on the runic wheel

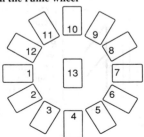

1 The self, the personality.
2 Money, possessions.
3 Family.
4 The home.
5 Creativity, self-expression.
6 The outside world, physical health.

7 Love and marriage.
8 Inheritance, death.
9 Education, travel.
10 Careers, social status.
11 Friendships, pleasure.
12 The inner life, psychic qualities.
13 The enquirer.

Rune interpretations

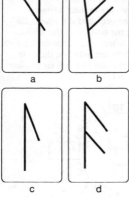

a *Upright* Be careful and plan ahead.
Reversed Impatience will lead to failure.
b *Upright* Romantic fulfilment.
Reversed Romantic difficulties.

c *Upright* Intuition, premonitions coming true.
Reversed Be cautious with money.
d *Upright* Old age, wisdom.
Reversed Bad advice, senility.

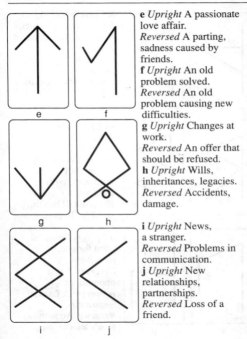

e *Upright* A passionate love affair.
Reversed A parting, sadness caused by friends.
f *Upright* An old problem solved.
Reversed An old problem causing new difficulties.
g *Upright* Changes at work.
Reversed An offer that should be refused.
h *Upright* Wills, inheritances, legacies.
Reversed Accidents, damage.
i *Upright* News, a stranger.
Reversed Problems in communication.
j *Upright* New relationships, partnerships.
Reversed Loss of a friend.

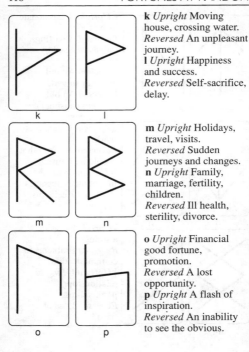

k *Upright* Moving house, crossing water. *Reversed* An unpleasant journey.
l *Upright* Happiness and success. *Reversed* Self-sacrifice, delay.

m *Upright* Holidays, travel, visits. *Reversed* Sudden journeys and changes.
n *Upright* Family, marriage, fertility, children. *Reversed* Ill health, sterility, divorce.

o *Upright* Financial good fortune, promotion. *Reversed* A lost opportunity.
p *Upright* A flash of inspiration. *Reversed* An inability to see the obvious.

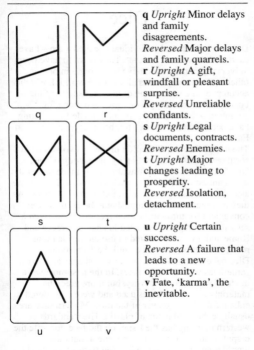

q *Upright* Minor delays and family disagreements.
Reversed Major delays and family quarrels.
r *Upright* A gift, windfall or pleasant surprise.
Reversed Unreliable confidants.
s *Upright* Legal documents, contracts.
Reversed Enemies.
t *Upright* Major changes leading to prosperity.
Reversed Isolation, detachment.

u *Upright* Certain success.
Reversed A failure that leads to a new opportunity.
v Fate, 'karma', the inevitable.

Dice

Dice – of which each individual is called a die – have existed since at least 2000BC. They seem to have been universally popular, and have been found in one or other of their many forms all over the world. Early dice accompanied a wide range of games, usually of the board-and-counters type, or were used alone for gambling – 'loaded' dice, specially made for cheating, have been found in ancient tombs in Egypt and the Far East.

The use of dice for divination probably evolved from sortilege, which is divination by the casting of lots. One form of sortilege, astragalomancy, made use of the direct ancestors of the dice we know today. These were astragals, the vertebrae or the ankle-bones of sheep. As they had four easily distinguishable faces, they were convenient for throwing – each face could be given a set value. Astragals were used in ancient Greece and Rome and, in fact, persisted in use alongside more recognisable forms of dice until the 10th century.

Dice have been made in a variety of shapes and sizes, sometimes with up to 20 faces. In the past most were made of wood, bone or ivory, but more precious materials were sometimes used and were considered to enhance the latent power of the dice. Modern dice are usually cubes and made of plastic. The standard western marking has the 1-spot on the face opposite the 6-spot, 2 opposite 5, and 3 opposite 4, but other numberings are still in use in other parts of the world.

Early dice
a Astragal.
b Ancient Egyptian die.
c Etruscan dice.
d Roman long die, marked *malest* (ill luck) on one side.
e Roman die with 14 faces.
f Die in the form of a six-sided figurine.
g Asian long dice.

ASTRAGALOMANCY

Today this is a form of divination using two dice, but
originally a pair of astragals (probably the left and right
ankle-bones of a sheep) would have been used. This
method allows you to use the dice to answer a specific
question. Concentrate on your question, and then throw
the dice into the circle. Add the numbers on the two
dice, and then consult the list of answers. If a die falls
outside the circle it is not counted.

One Yes.	**Seven** Have faith.
Two No.	**Eight** Be patient.
Three Take care.	**Nine** Certainly.
Four Be wise.	**Ten** Doubtful.
Five Good luck.	**Eleven** Nonsense.
Six Of course.	**Twelve** A chance.

READING THE DICE

Some people believe that the dice should be thrown
only on behalf of someone else, and not to predict your
own future. Another belief says that the dice should be
thrown in complete silence, and yet another holds that
cool weather and a calm atmosphere are the best
conditions for a good reading.

The most usual modern method is to draw a circle 12in
(30cm) in diameter on a table or other flat surface. You
then throw three dice out of your hand or from a cup to
land inside this circle. If all the dice land outside the
circle, pick them up and throw them again. If the same
should happen a second time, the dice should be
abandoned and you should wait for a more propitious
time – do not throw them a third time.

Add together the numbers on the three dice and look
up the meaning of the total. Any dice that fall outside

the circle are not counted. If one falls outside, add together the numbers on the other two, but remember that the die outside the circle means that your plans may go wrong. If two dice land outside the circle, trouble or a quarrel may be coming. If a die falls on the floor there are troubled times ahead, two dice on the floor suggest serious trouble. If one or more dice land outside the circle and the remaining dice in the circle total less than three, there is no reading – only the numbers from three to 18 are read.

If a number recurs during a reading, it indicates that significant news is on the way. In the rare event that one die lands on top of another and stays there, you may receive a gift – but you must also take care, both in business and in love.

Interpreting the totals

Three A surprise or some unexpected news may be on the way, but it will be favourable.

Four Disappointment or unpleasantness could be in store, and possibly bad luck, too.

Five Your wish will come true, but perhaps in an unexpected way. A stranger may bring happiness.

Six There will be loss and misfortune, probably in money and business matters.

Seven You will suffer setbacks and maybe unhappiness through scandal or gossip – be careful.

Eight Outside influences are strong, and you might be the victim of unfair blame or injustice.

Nine Lucky for love and marriage; you can expect reconciliation and forgiveness after a quarrel.

Ten A strong prediction of birth, also domestic happiness and a promotion or business success.

Eleven A parting, perhaps from someone close to you; there may be an illness.

Twelve Good news will arrive, probably by letter, and you should take advice before replying.

Thirteen This dark number predicts grief and sorrow, which may last a very long time.

Fourteen A friend will help you, or you may meet a new admirer or stranger who will become a close friend.

Fifteen You need to take great care, perhaps against some temptation into dishonesty.

Sixteen This number tells of travel, and the omens for the journey are very good.

Seventeen A change of plan may come about through a person from overseas or who is associated with water.

Eighteen This number is the best omen of all, bringing success, prosperity and happiness.

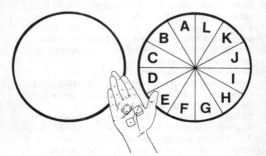

Dominoes

Dominoes are small, oblong-shaped tiles of wood, ivory or plastic. Each tile is divided in half, and each half has spots indicating numbers from zero to six. Modern sets consist of 28 tiles – one tile for every combination from double-blank to double-six. They are used to play a number of different games but, like dice, the numbers on the pieces can be used to predict the future.

Origins

Dominoes were first recorded in China in the 12th century BC, and these early examples would probably have been used for divination rather than for gaming. Dominoes are closely related to dice and may indeed have evolved as a form of dice for safe use in occult matters: using dice for both gambling and fortune telling could have been considered dangerous.

Dominoes are still used extensively for prediction in India and Korea, and some Indian and Chinese games combine gambling and fortune telling – certain tiles are thought to bring good luck even if the player loses a bet! In China the dominoes, like the dice, have red spots as well as black. A set of Chinese dominoes has 32 pieces: 11 identical pairs, 10 single dominoes and no blanks. European dominoes probably came from China, and appeared in Italy and France in the 18th century. Their name was probably derived from a long black cloak and face mask called a domino. French prisoners introduced dominoes into England at the end of the 18th century. The coloured spots and duplicate tiles were dropped in western sets, blanks were added and a 28-tile set in black with white spots became standard. Sets running up to nine-nine and even 12-12 do exist, but they are uncommon. In the move to the west some of the occult subtleties of dominoes were also lost: in the east the names given to the tiles – 'Leaping Gazelle', 'The Little Snakes' and so on – carry a strong mystic element.

HOW TO READ THE DOMINOES

Lay all the tiles face downward and shuffle them well. Draw three tiles, and read the meaning of each one. These interpretations must be organised into a coherent picture, and this will require imagination and subtlety on your part.

According to one method you should pick all three dominoes before looking at any of them, although you should re-shuffle the remaining tiles before each draw. Another way is to pick one domino and to consult its meaning. Then return the tile to the set and re-shuffle before picking for the second time. Repeat for the third draw. With this method you may draw the same tile more than once – if this happens, it presages a very quick fulfilment of the prophecy.

Whichever method you choose, it is important not to draw more than three dominoes at a consultation, or to consult the dominoes more than once a week, or it is said that the messages will become meaningless.

Domino meanings

Six-six This is the best domino in the set, with strong omens for success and happiness in every area of life.

Six-five A close friend or maybe a benefactor, but patience and perseverance are also indicated. A kind action will bring you great regard.

Six-four All the signs point to a quarrel, or maybe even a lawsuit, with an unsuccessful outcome.

Six-three You are going to travel, or a journey will affect your life. A holiday will be happy, and a journey may bring a gift.

Six-two Very good luck is coming your way, and your circumstances may be improved. But this tile is only lucky for the honest!

Six-one There will be an end to your problems. A good friend could be involved in this: a wedding is foretold.

Six-blank Be careful of false friends or a deceitful person. You could suffer some unhappiness because of gossip.

Five-five A strong omen for change, and the change will bring success. You might move to a new place where you will be happy, or make money from a new idea.

Five-four Profits and good fortune in material terms, possibly unexpected, but don't take any chances – it is not a good time for investments.

Five-three A calm and well-adjusted atmosphere here – you will get some good news or helpful advice from a visitor or from your boss.

Five-two A true friend will have an influence on your life, maybe because of his patience and tolerance. This is also an omen for birth.

Five-one A love affair, or an interesting meeting with a new friend, is in store. Things may not end happily for those in love.

Five-blank There will be some sadness– you may have to give comfort to a friend in trouble. But you need caution, so think carefully about what you say.

Four-four Happiness, fun, relaxation and celebration are the signs in this domino. There may be a party in a big building.

Four-three You might have expected some problems or disappointments, but instead you will find happiness and success.

Four-two A change of some sort, but not a happy one – setbacks, losses or maybe even a robbery. Someone you know is deceitful – be careful!

Four-one This domino is a sign that there will be some financial problems ahead – be sure that you pay any outstanding debts.

Four-blank Some news will not be favourable – you may be disappointed in a love affair, or something you want could be postponed. Try to reconcile a quarrel.

Three-three This domino predicts obstacles in your emotional life – jealousy or distress. But money is well favoured.

Three-two Some pleasant changes may be coming, but you need to be cautious just now, especially in financial matters.

Three-one The answer to the question in your mind is 'no'. Some surprising news might be useful, but beware of unhappiness caused by outsiders.

Three-blank This domino is not a good omen, and you could experience unexpected problems both at home and at work.

Two-two You will get what you want, as this is a good domino. Business success and personal happiness are predicted, but enemies might try to spoil it for you.

Two-one Financial problems and maybe a loss of money or property are indicated, but this domino is good for social life and old friends.

Two-blank This is a good omen for travel and meeting new friends, but something is worrying you and someone could cause difficulties for you.

One-one Harmony and affection are predicted, and a stranger could be involved. You have an important decision to make – don't put it off.

One-blank A stranger or outsider will bring some interesting news that could mean financial gain, but don't be too trusting.

Blank-blank This is the blackest domino in the set, and it carries the worst omens. The double blank will have a negative effect on all your activities.

Numerology

Numerology is believed to be one of the oldest forms of occult lore. Its origins cannot be traced, but the Babylonians, the ancient Egyptians, and many other peoples are all thought to have held theories of the occult significance of numbers. This concept is closely related to astrology, and to the observation of numbers found in natural phenomena – the five senses, the seven colours of the spectrum, the 12 signs of the zodiac and so on. Numbers were especially important to the Cabalists, both in ancient times and in the Middle Ages. The Cabala, the secret mystical lore of the Jews, contains a magico-philosophical science of numbers known as *gematria*, based on the 22 letters of the Hebrew alphabet.

The basis of numerology

Although there are some variations between the numerological systems that have come down to the present day, most seem to be based on the theories of the Greek mathematician and philosopher Pythagoras. He believed that the whole universe was ordered mathematically, and that as everything in it could be expressed in terms of numbers, numbers were therefore the key to the universe.

Numerology, which was also known as numeromancy or arithomancy, used to be practiced as a form of general divination; today its practitioners are mainly concerned with character analysis and potential. The basis of numerology is the belief that numbers – especially the primary numbers from 1 to 9 – exert an

influence on every facet of our lives and personalities.
Each person has numbers that relate to the significant
events in his life, the most important being the birth
number and the name number.

Personality

Many of the characteristics associated with the primary
numbers are related to personality, so allowing you to
assess the character of any individual whose name or
birth number you have calculated. When you use the
numbers for other purposes (for example, to find out if a
certain plan will be a good one) their meanings should
be interpreted according to their more general
characteristics.

Planets and days of the week

Each number is associated with a planet and with a
day of the week – said to be an auspicious day for
those whose birth number is linked with it. The
numbers also have positive connections with dates
containing the same number: for example, the 5th, 14th
and 23rd of each month are seen as good days for
anyone whose birth number is 5.

PRIMARY AND SECONDARY NUMBERS

Finding the primary number

The primary numbers from 1 to 9 are the basis of all
numerological systems. Every number can be reduced
to its primary by a simple process of left-to-right
addition. Thus 25 becomes 2+5=7, and 7 is its primary
number. Similarly, 198 becomes 1+9+8=18, which is
further reduced to 1+8=9. The same simple process can
be applied to dates, names (by a system of number-letter
equivalents, shown on next page), events and so on.

All numerologists agree about the fundamental importance of the primary numbers, but some also offer meanings for secondary numbers (i.e. 10 and above). The secondary numbers, if used, are also arrived at by a process of addition.

1 2 3 4 5 6 7 8 9 0

Birth numbers

Your most important number is your birth number. This is calculated by adding up the numbers of your date of birth. For example, if you were born on June 11, 1952, add 6 (because June is the sixth month) +1+1+1+9+5+2, which gives 25. Then add 2+5, giving 7. Number 7 is therefore your birth number. This number is of course unchangeable, and it shows the numerical influence at birth. By looking up the meanings ascribed to 7, you can find your natural characteristics and basic personality traits.

Name numbers

To find your name number, convert the letters of your name to figures, using number-letter equivalents. You should work from the name you usually use, not necessarily your full, formal name. For example, using the older system of equivalents, Jenny Brown becomes

J E N N Y
1+5+5+5+1 = 17, 1+7 = 8

B R O W N
2+2+7+6+5 =22, 2+2 = 4

8+4 = 12, 1+2 = 3

Jenny Brown's name number is therefore 3.

A person's name number tends to show acquired or
developed traits, and unlike the birth number, it can of
course be changed. It is considered ideal if a person's
birth and name numbers coincide; this will reinforce
the characteristics of the birth number, but in a
harmonious way. If there is a serious mismatch
between the two numbers, it may indicate inner
conflicts that remain unresolved. Let us suppose that
Jenny Brown has a birth number of 9. Although 3 is
not unharmonious with 9, Jenny might find that she
enjoyed more success in her life if she used her full
name, Jennifer, because Jennifer Brown gives a name
number of 9 to match her birth number.

Number-letter equivalents

The older system of number-letter equivalents below
omits the number 9. It was omitted because it was held
to be of special significance; in the Cabalistic tradition
it was considered to be the numerical equivalent of the
name of God.

1	2	3	4	5	6	7	8
A	B	C	D	E	U	O	F
I	K	G	M	H	V	Z	P
Q	R	L	T	N	W		
J		S			X		
Y							

1	2	3	4	5	6	7	8	9
A	B	C	D	E	F	G	H	I
J	K	L	M	N	O	P	Q	R
S	T	U	V	W	X	Y	Z	

The more modern system of equivalents above uses all the primary numbers, including the number 9.

NUMEROLOGICAL ANALYSIS

If possible, begin your analysis with the birth number. It represents your subject's inborn characteristics and is known as the 'number of personality'. Next analyse the name number for the name by which your subject is best known. It shows the traits developed during life, and is known as the 'number of development'. If your subject uses another name at work – initials instead of a first name, perhaps, or a stage name – calculate its number as well: it shows your subject's achievements, and is called the 'number of attainment'.

Your subject's inner nature is shown by the vowel number, known as the 'number of underlying influence'. It is found by adding up the number equivalents of the vowels in a name and reducing them to the primary. Finally, take into account any number that occurs frequently and strongly when you are calculating the birth, name and vowel numbers. This is the frequency number, which has a modifying effect on the analysis, and is known as the 'number of added influence'.

The secondary numbers

Some numerologists take into account the meanings of the secondary numbers as well as the nine primaries. There are many ways to do this, as well as many different interpretations of the secondary numbers themselves. Normally a secondary number will be taken into account only as additional information, or to add a further dimension to the interpretation of the primary number. Suppose, for example, that the letters of a name add up to 11 (which when further reduced gives a name number of 2), and the person's birthday falls on November 11. Such a strong coincidence of the number 11 (November is the 11th month) cannot be ignored, although 11 is not the occult primary birth or name number. The implications of 11 can be added to the meanings of the primary to fill out the total picture. The more mystically minded numerologists have offered a vast list of meanings for secondary numbers. Another school of thought recognises only the secondary numbers up to 22 (there are 22 letters in the Hebrew alphabet). More often, however, just a few significant secondaries are taken into account, as listed below.

11, 12, 13, 22, 40

11 This is the number of special mystical awareness, possibly balanced between good and evil.

12 A powerful sign of completeness, being the number of signs of the zodiac, the months, the apostles etc.

13 One more than the 'perfect 12', this number is usually associated with ill fortune and the black arts, but it can also be a positive force.

22 This number, like 12, has a strong sense of fullness and completeness. It is the number of letters in the Hebrew alphabet, and of the cards in the major arcana of the tarot.

40 Another potent number suggesting completeness.

Interpreting the numbers

1 Number 1 stands for the Sun, and all that is strong, individual and creative. Number 1 people are born leaders; they are ambitious and active, and often dominant and aggressive. This is a powerful number, and it augurs success. It is the number of innovators, leaders, winners – but also of tyrants! Number 1 people can be very self-centred, ruthless and stubborn if crossed, and their chosen career or activity will probably receive more energy and attention than their personal relationships. Sunday is the day associated with the Sun and with the number 1.

2 The Moon, and Monday, are associated with the number 2. Number 2 people are more gentle, passive and artistic than the stronger number 1 characters. Number 2s are more geared to thought than to action, and although they are inventive, they will be less forceful in carrying out their plans. They are likely to have charm and powers of intuition, but they may suffer from a lack of self-confidence. Number 2 people can be changeable – perhaps even deceitful – and may be over-sensitive and depressive. Number 2 people get on well with their opposites, the number 1 people.

3 Energetic, disciplined, talented, number 3 people often achieve success in their chosen fields. In fact, they are seldom satisfied with less, as they are conscientious, very proud and independent, and they love to be in control. They may be too fond of telling other people what to do, but they have many good qualities. A superficial show may hide considerable spirituality, since 3 is the number of the Trinity. Number 3 people have good relationships with other 3s, and those born under 6 and 9. Jupiter is the planet of this number, and Thursday is the luckiest day for number 3 people.

1☉ **2**☽ **3**♃ **4**♅

5☿ **6**♀ **7**♆ **8**♄ **9**♂

4 Number 4 – number of the seasons, the elements, the points of the compass – is oriented to the earth, and its people may be steady and practical, with great endurance. Yet number 4 – the square – contains its own opposite, and number 4 people often see everything from the opposite point of view, making them rebellious and unconventional. They are seldom interested in material things. Making friends is hard for 4s, and they may feel isolated. People whose numbers are 1, 2, 7 and 8 are the best friends or partners for 4s. Number 4 is associated with the planet Uranus, and with Sunday.

5 Number 5 – the number of the senses – symbolises the planet Mercury, and people born under this number are mercurial in all their characteristics. Lively, sensual, pleasure-seeking, impulsive, quick-thinking and quick-tempered, these highly strung number 5 people may have trouble with their nerves. They are good at making money, especially by risk or

speculation, and they bounce back easily from any
failure. They make friends easily with people born
under any other number, but close friends will probably
be fellow number 5s. Wednesday is the luckiest day for
the quicksilver number 5.

6 A 'perfect' number because it is the sum of its factors
(1, 2, 3), 6 is balanced and harmonious, and is
associated with family love and domesticity. Number 6
people are very reliable and trustworthy, but they may
also be obstinate. Their planet, Venus, governs
devotion in love, but number 6 people are romantic
rather than sensual. They have a great love of beauty;
they are usually attractive and have a greater ability to
make friends than any other number. Despite a hatred
of any sort of discord, they can be obstinate fighters.
Their luckiest day is Friday.

7 Number 7 is thought to have occult significance, and
people born under its influence often have a strongly
philosophical or spiritual outlook – they are not usually
interested in material things. They may be highly
intuitive, even psychic. Number 7 people often exert a
mysterious influence over others, but may also have a
tendency to become too introverted. They are original
thinkers, and have the luck associated with their
number. Their planet is Neptune, which is associated
with water, and number 7 people often have a restless
love of travel and of the sea. Monday is their luckiest
day.

8 Number 8 is a strange, difficult number. It is twice 4,
and so incorporates the rebellious contradictions of that
number. Number 8 may mean sorrow, yet it is also
associated with worldly success. Number 8 people

have great willpower and individuality, but they may appear cold. In fact they have deep and intense feelings, and are often misunderstood by others. Their planet is Saturn, and Saturday is their most important day.

9 Number 9 is sometimes considered the ultimate number, with special or even sacred significance. When multiplied by any number, it reproduces itself (e.g. 3x9=27, 2+7=9). Number 9 symbolises the planet Mars, and its people are fighters – active and determined, they usually succeed after a struggle, but they are also prone to accident and injury, and may be quarrelsome. But at its best, number 9 will influence the highest qualities of courage and brotherly love. Number 9 people should try to carry out their plans on Tuesday, the day governed by their planet, Mars.

Common omens and superstitions

Some omens – today we call them superstitions – have been passed down from ancient times. The correct interpretation of signs from the gods used to be the province of the augurs and other soothsayers, but some of their knowledge became common property and has since passed into folklore. Other superstitions have grown up because, say, an unusual occurrence led to a particular piece of good or bad luck, or because a fairly common occurrence seemed always to be followed by a particular type of weather (usually rain).

Walking under a ladder has long been believed to bring bad luck. The Egyptian god Osiris was said to have ascended to the sky by means of a ladder, as was the ancient Persian god Mithras, who was later much worshipped by the soldiers of the Roman army. Since ladders were so much in use by the gods, walking under them became taboo for humans in order to prevent the gods becoming angry.

Salt, too, was precious to the gods – and to humans, as it was an important trade commodity. It was sprinkled on the heads of animals to be sacrificed, and was used in the making of solemn and binding agreements. Spilling salt was unlucky in many ways: it offended the gods, was a sign of broken faith and, on a more mundane level, was a waste of money.

Omens and their interpretations can vary considerably from country to country, and can even be completely reversed in their meaning. The commonest example of this is probably the black cat: if one crosses your path it is regarded as lucky in England, but is considered unlucky in other parts of Europe and in the USA.

Omens of good luck

Bats flying at twilight.
A gift of a hive of bees.
A robin flying into the house.
A white butterfly.
A four-leaved clover.
Hearing crickets singing.
Burning your fingernail parings.
Cutting your hair during a storm.
Finding a hairpin and hanging it on a hook.
Seeing a load of hay.
Looking at the new moon over your right shoulder.
Picking up a nail that was pointing towards you.
Picking up a pencil found in the street.
Keeping a piece of oyster shell in your pocket.
Carrying a rabbit's foot.
Walking in the rain.
Sleeping on unironed sheets.
Spilling your drink while proposing a toast.
Breaking uncoloured glass other than a mirror.
Sleeping facing south.
A sprig of white heather.
Meeting sheep.
A ladybird.
A bluebird.
A strange dog following you home.
Putting your dress on inside out.
Rubbing two horseshoes together.
A peapod containing nine peas.

A horseshoe.
Picking up a pin.
A wishbone.
Catching two rats in the same trap.
Sneezing three times before breakfast.
Meeting a chimney-sweep.

Omens of rain
Bats hitting a building.
Bees staying in the hive.
A frog croaking in the daytime.
Killing a spider.
A crescent moon upside down.
A halo around the moon.
A rainbow on a Saturday.
Smoke accumulating close to the ground.
Snakes crawling to higher ground.
A spade stuck in the ground.
An itching corn.
Dropping a piece of buttered bread.
Burning ferns.
Cattle lying down.
Leaves turning up.
A red sky in the morning.
Donkeys braying.
Cocks crowing in the evening.
Soot falling down the chimney.

Omens of bad luck
Emptying ashes after dark.
A bat entering the house.
Putting a hat on a bed.
An owl hooting three times.
Wearing an opal unless you were born in October.

Singing before breakfast.
Giving away a wedding present.
Borrowing, lending or burning a broom.
A five-leaved clover.
Bringing eggs into the house after dark.
Cutting your nails on Friday.
Dropping a glove.
Bringing white lilac or hawthorn blossom into a house.
Looking at the new moon over your left shoulder.
Taking anything out of the house on New Year's Day.
Peacock feathers.
Removing your wedding ring.
A rooster crowing at night.
Killing a seagull.
Mending a garment while you are wearing it.
Putting shoes on a chair or table.
Dropping an umbrella.
Seeing an owl in daytime.
Keeping your slippers on a shelf above head height.
Putting an umbrella on a table.
Blossom and fruit growing together on the same branch
(except on orange trees).
Meeting a hare on the road.
Violets flowering out of season.
Meeting a pig immediately after a wedding.
Meeting a grave-digger.
Buttoning a button into the wrong buttonhole.
Opening an umbrella indoors.
Putting on your left shoe before your right.
Sitting on a table without keeping one foot on the
ground.
Killing a cricket.

A picture falling.

Breaking your glass when proposing a toast.

Putting your shirt on inside out.

Getting out of bed left foot first.

Putting a pair of bellows on a table.

A ring breaking on your finger.

Three butterflies together.

Red and white flowers in the same arrangement.

Bringing Christmas greenery into the house before December 24.

Leaving Christmas decorations up after Twelfth Night.

1 HORSES (HIPPOMANCY)

One white horse Ill luck.

One white horse seen by a pair of lovers Good luck.

Two white horses together Good luck.

A piebald horse Good fortune.

The tail of a piebald horse Misfortune.

2 CATS (AILUROMANCY)

A cat washing its face or ears Rain.

A cat washing one ear three times Expect visitors from the direction in which the cat is looking.

A cat following you Money.

A cat climbing the furniture Rain.

A cat that unaccountably leaves home Disaster.

A grey cat Good luck.

A black cat entering your house Good luck.

A black cat crossing your path Lucky in Britain; unlucky in the USA and some European countries.

A white cat crossing your path Illness.

A black cat walking under a ladder Bad luck for the next person to climb the ladder.

A cat sneezing on the day before a wedding Unlucky for the bride in the USA; lucky for her elsewhere.

Cat appearing around a door Think of a question and call for your cat. If his right paw appears first around the door, the answer to your question is yes. If the left paw is first, the answer is no.

Meeting three black cats in succession Good luck.

Cat sleeping with its back to the fire Rain.

3 SPIDERS (ARACHNOMANCY)

Seeing a spider in the morning Grief.

Seeing a spider at noon Anxiety.

Seeing a spider in the evening Financial loss.

Seeing a spider spinning a web Some sources say this indicates that there is a plot against you, others that you will receive a gift, probably new clothes.

Seeing a spider spinning in the morning Good luck.

Seeing a spider spinning in the afternoon A journey.

Finding a spider's web in a doorway A visitor.

Seeing a spider climbing its thread Good news.

Seeing a spider dropping on its thread Good luck, unless it reaches the floor, when it is bad luck.

Finding a spider on your clothes Money, a letter or both.

Finding a spider on your body Good fortune.

Finding a small red 'spider' Money.

Killing a spider Bad luck.

Seeing a spider cross a wall Good luck.

4 KNIVES AND SCISSORS

Dropping a knife on the floor   4
A male visitor.

Dropping a pair of scissors
A disappointment, which can be averted by stepping on the scissors before picking them up.

Scissors landing point down when dropped Illness.

Crossed knives Bad luck.

Breaking a pair of scissors Bad luck.

A knife left blade upward Danger.

Giving a gift of a knife or scissors
This can cut the friendship unless a pin or a penny is given in exchange.

A new knife used first on anything other than paper or wood Bad luck.

Scissors hanging on a hook Good luck.

Placing or finding a knife in the cradle of a newborn child Good luck.

5 MEANING OF ITCHES

1 Top of head Promotion, good luck.

2 Left cheek or left ear Compliments.

3 Right cheek or right ear Derogatory remarks.

4 Left eye Disappointment.

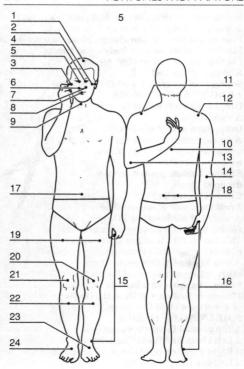

5 Right eye A meeting.
6 Inside nose Grief, bad luck.
7 Outside nose 'Crossed, vexed, or kissed by a fool'.
8 Mouth Insults.
9 Neck Illness.
10 Back Disappointment.
11 Left shoulder Unhappiness.
12 Right shoulder An inheritance.
13 Left elbow Bad news.
14 Right elbow Good news.
15 Left palm or left ankle Bills to pay.
16 Right palm or right ankle Expect money.
17 Abdomen An invitation.
18 Loins A reconciliation.
19 Thighs A move.
20 Left knee Gossip.
21 Right knee Good news.
22 Shins An unpleasant surprise.
23 Left foot An unprofitable journey.
24 Right foot A profitable journey.

6 LAMPADOMANCY

This involves taking the omens from a single oil lamp, or from a torch flame.

Flame with a single point Good luck.
Flame with two points Bad luck.
Flame with three points Good luck.
Flame bending Illness.
Flame unexpectedly extinguished Disaster.

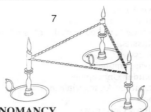

7 LYCHNOMANCY

This is divination from the flames of three wax
candles. Arrange the three candles in an equilateral
triangle and light a fourth candle some distance away
to provide enough light for the reading. Switch off all
the other lights in the room, and light the three candles
from one match. Read the omens from the appearance
of their flames.

A flame wavering from side to side Travel.

One flame burning brighter than the others Great
success.

A glow or radiance at the tip of the wick Prosperity.

A curling or spiralling flame Enemies plotting.

Sparks Be cautious.

**Rising and falling flames, or candles burning
unevenly** Danger.

Flame spluttering Disappointment.

Flame unexpectedly extinguished Great misfortune.

8 LITHOMANCY

This is divination using precious stones, one form of
which involves candlelight. Scatter gemstones of
different colours around a candle. Darken the room,
light the candle, close your eyes and clear your mind of

thoughts. When you open your eyes, notice which colour of stone first reflects the light back to you. (In the absence of a good selection of gems, coloured glass beads can be used as an alternative.)

Colourless Success and happiness.

Red Romance.

Dark red A wedding.

Yellow Infidelity.

Green A wish will come true.

Turquoise An unexpected opportunity.

Blue Good luck.

Violet Grief.

Purple A quarrel.

Black Ill luck.

OTHER CANDLE OMENS

a A candle burning with a tall straight flame Expect the arrival of a stranger.

b A dripping candle A drip of wax on the side of a candle indicates ill luck for the person sitting on that side.

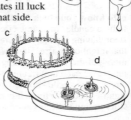

c Birthday cake candles Your cake should carry a lighted candle for each year of your age. Make a wish, and try to blow out all the candles in one breath. If you succeed, the wish will come true.

d To know if your lover is true Take two halves of a walnut shell, two small candles or wax matches and a bowl of water. Stand a candle upright in each half of the walnut shell, fixing it into place with a little melted wax. Set the walnut shell boats in the middle of the bowl of water, naming one candle for yourself, and the other for your lover. Light the candles. If the two boats float side by side with the candles burning evenly, you will be true to each other. If the boats drift apart, overturn or the flame goes out, the relationship is doomed. If your candle burns for longer than that named for your lover, then you love more than you are loved, and vice versa.

e To know your luck for the next year Arrange 12 lighted candles in a large circle on a wood or concrete floor, having first carefully removed any furnishings that might catch fire. Name a candle in turn for each month of the year. Beginning at the January candle, jump over each in turn until you have completed the circle. Any candle knocked over or extinguished signifies bad luck for that particular month; a candle still burning indicates good luck.

Food

Many of the special days that punctuate our calendar –
Twelfth Night, Candlemas, May Day and so on – date
from pagan times, although they have since been
absorbed into the Christian tradition. They would have
been, and in some cases still are, holidays when food
and feasting played an important part. So it is not
surprising that many of the forms of prediction
involving food are supposed to work best on one or
other of these feast days.

Halloween, on October 31, was the pagan New Year's
Eve. As such, it was an important time for attempting
to discover the future. It was also the day dedicated to
Pomona, the Roman goddess of the orchards, and so
apples came to play an important part in the Halloween
divination rites – most of which are concerned with
whom and when you will wed.

The details of some of the forms of divination that
involve food have been lost in history. Crithomancy,
for example, involved reading the markings on freshly
baked bread or cakes. And tyromancy was divination
from cheese. Alphitomancy enabled the seers to detect
lies or dishonesty with special cakes made of wheat or
barley flour – these were supposed to be swallowed
easily by those of a clear conscience, but to choke liars
or wrong-doers. A similar ordeal was known in
medieval English law, but the special cakes were
replaced by a consecrated 'trial slice' of bread and
cheese.

ONIONS (CROMNIOMANCY)

To make a wish come true Wish while burning onion skins on the fire.

To find the name of the person you will marry Label several onions with different names and leave them to sprout. The first to sprout reveals the name of your future partner.

To answer a question Attach the possible alternative answers to your question to several onions; the first onion to sprout will give the answer to your question. Traditionally the onions were placed on a church altar on Christmas Eve.

APPLES

To know the initial of the name of your future partner Peel an apple carefully, keeping the peel in one long piece. Then:

(a) count off the twists by calling out the letters of the alphabet, and the last letter you call will be the initial of the name; or

(b) throw the piece of peel over your left shoulder and see which initial it most resembles.

To know the initial of the name of the next person to visit you Cut an apple into nine pieces, and throw the last piece over your left shoulder while reciting the alphabet aloud. The letter you have reached when the piece of apple touches the floor will be the initial.

Wishing on an apple Cut an apple in half through the center while you make a wish. If you have cut the apple without cutting any of the pips your wish will come true.

Apple breaking as you eat it Bad luck.

Bobbing for apples Fill a bowl with water, and cast in

several apples. Several people at a time should attempt to secure an apple with their lips and teeth – hands may not be used. The first person to secure an apple will be the first to marry. If the apples are of different sizes, the prosperity you can expect in your life will be indicated by the relative size of your apple – the larger the apple, the more prosperous your life. An alternative form of bobbing is for each woman present to make a secret mark on her apple before casting it into the bowl. The men then bob for the apples to find out which of the women present they will marry.

To know when you will marry Several people each tie an apple to a piece of string, and then whirl them around. Whoever has the apple that falls off the string first will marry first; whoever owns the last apple to fall will not marry at all.

To see your future partner On Halloween sit alone in front of a mirror, combing your hair and eating an apple. You will see in the mirror a reflection of your future partner looking over your left shoulder. Alternatively, cut the apple into nine pieces and eat eight of them with your back to a mirror. Then throw the ninth piece over your left shoulder and turn quickly to look in the glass. You should be able to see the reflection of your future partner.

PUDDINGS AND CAKES

Christmas pudding A small silver coin is stirred into the mixture before the pudding is cooked. Finding the coin in your slice of pudding means prosperity for the next year. Alternatively, a variety of charms are included in the pudding, and your future depends on the charm you find – a horseshoe for luck, perhaps, or a ring for a wedding.

Twelfth Night cake Keep a piece in a dry place for three months. If it has not become mouldy, good fortune will be yours for the rest of the year.

Dreaming bannock On Shrove Tuesday evening, bake a bannock (a traditional unleavened oatcake) and include in the mixture some small silver charms and a silver ring. There must be complete silence during the mixing and cooking. As soon as the bannock is ready, cut it into as many pieces as there are unmarried people present. Your future for the next 12 months will be shown by the type of charm you find. The piece of bannock should not be eaten, but wrapped in your left sock or stocking, and placed under your pillow. You should then dream of your future partner.

Dumb cake On Midsummer's Eve, three people together mix, knead and bake a cake from flour and water, with a little added sugar. The cake is then broken into three, and each person breaks their third into nine pieces. All the pieces are then passed through a wedding ring, borrowed from someone who has worn it for at least three years. Each person eats their nine pieces of cake, and the wedding ring is hung over the bed in which they should all sleep. Dreams of their future partners should then follow – providing that they have carried out the entire ritual in total silence.

Wedding cake Fast throughout Friday, and then fall asleep with a piece of wedding cake under your pillow. You should then dream of your future partner. Alternatively, if you wish to know if you will marry a particular person, pass the wedding cake three times through a borrowed wedding ring. Wrap the cake in a

piece of paper on which you have written the name of
the person concerned, and sleep with it under your
pillow. You should then dream of your future partner.

NUTS

To dream of the occupation of your future partner
Chop finely together a single walnut and a single
hazelnut, and grate a piece of nutmeg. Mix them all
together with a little dough or damp bread, form the
mixture into nine small pills, and swallow all of them
before going to bed. Your dreams are then said to show
you a clear symbol of your future partner's occupation.
To know if your lover is true Place two nuts in the
embers of a fire, or on the bars of the grate, naming one
nut for yourself and one for your lover. If the nuts burn
quietly together, the relationship will be a long and
happy one. If, however, the nuts flare up fiercely,
explode or jump away from one another, the
relationship will be ended by the person whose nut
flares up or jumps away first.

EGGS

Egg whites Pour an egg white into a wine glass that is
about three-quarters full of water. Place your hand on
top of the glass, and swirl the mixture around gently.
Leave it to stand for some time. The white will have
formed into shaped clots from which it is possible for
you to read your future.
Egg rolling On Easter Day, several people should take
coloured hard-boiled eggs to the top of a sloping grassy
field. Each person should mark an egg with an
identifying mark, and then roll it down the hill. Those
whose eggs reach the bottom unscathed will have good
luck for the next year; those whose eggs break can

expect misfortune. If all the eggs are released at the same time, the first egg to reach the bottom of the hill intact indicates the person who will marry first.

LETTUCE

When you are dressing a green salad, the number of lettuce leaves that fall from the bowl as you are tossing them in the dressing will tell you the number of years before you marry.

PEAS AND BEANS

On Care Sunday (the fifth Sunday in Lent, now called Passion Sunday) hide a small bean in a large dish of peas to be served with the main meal. The person who finds the bean on their plate will be the first to marry.

Geomancy

Although geomancy properly means divination by the
earth, the 'earth' in question is usually sand, dust or dry
soil. Arab geomancers have interpreted the patterns
made when a handful of sand or dust was cast onto a
smooth surface; Navaho wise men have allowed the
sand to trickle through their fingers into prophetic
patterns on the ground; and some African witch doctors
have read the marks made by a crab scrambling around
in a bowl of wet sand. Newer methods involve the
interpretation of random marks made in the sand with a
pointer – a process similar to automatic writing.

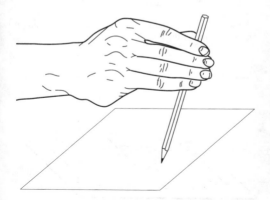

READING THE SAND

Spread out some fine, dry sand or soil in a tray, or on a
flat space on the ground. You will need some form of
pointer to make marks on the sand – a sharp stick,
perhaps, or even a pencil. Sit in silence, either in
complete darkness, or with a blindfold around your
eyes. The querant should sit next to you, concentrating
on the question to be answered.

Rest your wrist on the edge of the tray, with the tip of
the pointer just touching the sand. Clear your mind of
all thoughts, and allow the pointer to move of its own
accord. Only inspect the omens on the tray when you
are sure that the pointer has finished moving.

Letters, parts of words or complete words may have
been formed, or you may see a series of symbols.

A rough timescale can be established by considering
the whole width of the sand as one year, and dividing it
into sections for the months.

M, m (a) Maybe.
N, n No.
P, p Perhaps.
Y, y Yes.
Short, separated lines Lack of purpose.
Short, deep line A visitor.
Long, deep line A journey.
Small, scattered crosses (b) Dissension and conflict.
Large cross Love affair (happy if distinct, unhappy if indistinct).
Small circle Coming marriage.
Large circle (c) Misfortune at hand.
Triangle Successful career.
Square Protection.
Birds News, travel.
Mountain Fame, a move or change.
House Stability.
Sword (d) Success and peace if pointing upward; failure or illness if pointing downward.

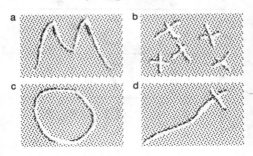

In the absence of sand, marks can be made on paper with a pen or pencil. In paper geomancy, the diviner exerts the minimum of control over his pencil while it makes four groups of four rows of random points. The points in each row are then counted: an even number in a row is represented by two dots, an odd number by one dot. This converts each group of four rows into one of 16 possible shapes made out of dots (shown) whose Latin names (translated) probably date from the 13th century. Some diviners choose to interpret these shapes as they stand. Others prefer to manipulate them according to a complex set of rules, translating some shapes into others, and interpreting the resulting patterns in the light of their relationship with the 12 astrological houses.

DOTS ON PAPER

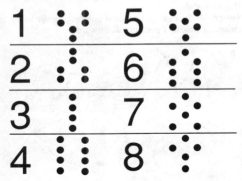

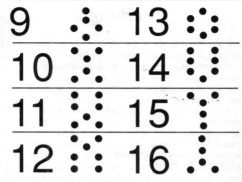

1 **Fortuna major** Great good fortune.
2 **Fortuna minor** Less good fortune.
3 **Via** Way.
4 **Populus** People, nation.
5 **Acquisitio** To seek, to gain.
6 **Laetitia** Happiness.
7 **Amissio** Loss.
8 **Puella** Girl.
9 **Puer** Boy.
10 **Conjunctio** Joining, meeting.
11 **Albus** White.
12 **Rubeus** Red.
13 **Carcer** Prison.
14 **Tristitia** Sadness.
15 **Caput draconis** Dragon's head.
16 **Cauda draconis** Dragon's tail.

Scrying

Scrying is divination by gazing into a reflecting
surface. No-one knows when or where it began, but it
has a long history in nearly all the world's cultures.
Almost any reflecting surface can and has been used at
one time or another – water, glass, polished metal,
precious stones, blood, even soap bubbles.

Scrying has links with hydromancy, because at first
water and other liquids were the most important and
the most easily available reflectors. The water could be
a sacred pool or spring (a form of divination called
pegomancy), or a liquid could be held in a special
container. The Babylonians gazed into liquids in sacred
bowls; the Egyptians into a pool of ink in the hand; the
Hindus into bowls of molasses; and the Greeks lowered
mirrors into sacred fountains and springs.

Mirror-gazing (catoptromancy) is another form of
scrying. The earliest mirrors were of polished metal,
and were often decorated on the non-reflecting side.
The ancient Chinese, for example, had polished bronze
mirrors decorated with cosmological and astrological
symbols, and looked in them for the reflections of
demons. Witches in the 14th century were said to use
mirrors of polished onyx to speak to spirits. But by the
late Middle Ages, when mirror-gazing was at the
height of its popularity, many of the mirrors would
have been of the silvered glass with which we are
familiar today; catoptromancers were recommended to
expose their mirrors to the lunar rays before staring at
the reflection of the moonlight in the glass. (Even

today we have superstitions that involve gazing into a mirror by moonlight in the hope of seeing your future marriage partner.)

But the most widespread and popular form of scrying is crystallomancy – crystal-gazing. Crystal balls have been known in Europe since about the 15th century, but they were also used by the Mayans and Incas, by North American Indians and Australian aborigines and by tribes in Borneo, New Guinea and Madagascar.

NOSTRADAMUS

Michel de Notredame (1503-1566), known as Nostradamus, is probably the most famous seer of all time. His prophecies – all published during his lifetime – were later interpreted as being predictions of the Great Fire of London in 1666, the French Revolution, Napoleon's defeat at Waterloo, Hitler's rise to power and its consequences, the atom bomb attacks on Hiroshima and Nagasaki and much more. Although Nostradamus was a noted astrologer, most of his published prophecies were obtained by scrying. His preferred method seems to have been to gaze into a brass bowl of water resting on a brass tripod, but he is also known to have used a looking glass to see the futures of specific individuals. He wrote his prophecies in quatrains (four-line verses) in a mixture of French, Latin and words of his own invention, decorated them with puns and

anagrams, and employed initials, abbreviations and
nicknames when referring to people.

SIMPLE CATOPTROMANCY

To know how long it will be until you marry Look at
the reflection of a full moon in a hand mirror, preferably
one that is silver-backed. The years to your wedding can
be estimated from the length of time that passes before
you see a cloud obscuring the moon or a bird flying
across it.

To see your future partner Look into a mirror at
midnight on Halloween while holding a lighted candle
and you should see the reflection of your future partner
looking over your left shoulder.

CRYSTALLOMANCY

The lamen

Some crystallomancers believe that the crystal should be
supported on an ornate circular table called the lamen,
which stands within a magic circle. Both the top of the
lamen (**A**) and the magic circle on the floor (**B**) are
engraved with mystic names. The pedestal supporting
the crystal bears the name SADAY, and is flanked by two
candlesticks engraved ELOHIM and ELOHE respectively.
Other crystallomancers feel that this ritual is unnecessary,
and that a simple black cloth to prevent any reflections
in the crystal is all that is required.

Using the crystal

The experts recommend the use of a sphere about 4in
(10cm) in diameter, made of beryl or quartz crystal. You
may prefer to use a glass sphere instead, but you should
ensure that it is free of any blemishes or bubbles that
might distract you.

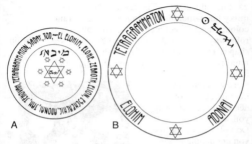

A B

You are the only person who should handle your crystal ball. Wash it in vinegar and water, polish it with a velvet cloth or a chamois leather and keep it wrapped up when you are not using it. Always keep it away from extremes of heat and cold and do not allow the direct light of the sun to fall on it, as this is said to ruin the susceptibility of the crystal. Moonlight, however, is said to be beneficial.

Sit in a north-facing room: there should be just enough light to read by. Not more than two other people should be in the room with you, and they must sit quietly, at least an arm's length away. Hold the crystal in your hand or place it on a small stand on a table. A black background – a cloth on the table and a curtain behind the crystal – will aid your concentration and act as a background for your images. Or, if you prefer, you can support the crystal on the traditional lamen within its mystic circle of names. Sit still, empty your mind and gaze into the crystal. The crystal should fill with a milky hue which then changes through a range of colours until it becomes black. This blackness will then roll away and reveal the images. You may see symbolic shapes and coloured clouds, which you will need to interpret. Or you may see moving, sequential images – as if you were watching a film – in which case you need only report what you see.

Do not worry if at first you are unable to see anything in the crystal. Scrying is said to come easily to only about one person in 20 – people who are psychically sensitive and receptive, with powers of perfect concentration. Other people will need practice and perseverance to develop any latent powers. Remember that you can practice scrying with very simple materials – a mirror, perhaps, or a glass of water.

CLOUDS IN THE CRYSTAL
White clouds Good fortune.
Black clouds Ill fortune.
Violet, green or blue clouds Joy.
Red, orange or yellow clouds Danger, trouble, difficulty.
Ascending clouds An affirmative reply to your question.
Descending clouds A negative reply to your question.
Clouds moving to the right Spirits present.
Clouds moving to the left Spirits have departed.

SYMBOLS IN THE CRYSTAL
Anchor Safety, hope.
Beetle Long life.
Bird A message.
Crown Glory, responsibility.
Eye Good fortune, forethought, but can be a symbol of evil.
Frog Fertility, something beneficial but hidden.
Fruit Children.
Globe Travel.
Heart pierced by a dagger Suffering.
Lighthouse Danger ahead, but there is hope.
Mask Deceit, tragedy.
Scales Justice, even-handedness – or the reverse.
Skull Death, wisdom.
Snake Health, knowledge, temptation.
Star Success, but be careful.
Swords A quarrel.
Water-lily Creativity.

EVENTS OCCURRING IN THE CRYSTAL

If at front of crystal Events relate to the present or the immediate future.

If at back of crystal Events relate to the remote past or the distant future.

If to your left Events are real.

If to your right Events are symbolic.

MENTAL ATTITUDE

Whichever your preferred form of scrying – a crystal ball (**a**), a mirror (**b**), or a bowl of liquid (**c**) – the correct mental attitude will be an important factor. In the past, crystallomancers and catoptromancers have adopted elaborate rituals to prepare themselves and to create the right atmosphere of inner tranquillity and calm. Your own personal rituals will evolve in time – you may, for example, find that some form of meditation helps to clear your mind before you begin scrying.

Tasseography

Reading the teacups (tasseography) probably began with the ancient Chinese. They were accustomed to taking omens from the appearance of the inside of bells – and their handleless teacups, when inverted, looked very like small bells. So the teacups became associated with the bell omens, and the patterns formed by the tea-leaves inside the cups came to have a divinatory significance.

Of course, if you dislike tea you can always read the grounds left in the bottom of your coffee cup, or the residue left by any other drink – the Romans, for example, read the lees of their wine. Because it results from both personal and random factors, the pattern made by the sediment left at the bottom of any drinking cup has always been considered of great importance in predicting the drinker's future, no matter what the original contents.

MOLYBDOMANCY AND CEROMANCY

Other societies have used other methods to produce symbols similar to those found in the tea-leaves. In medieval times, molten tin or lead was dripped into cold water to produce the characteristic shapes. This method, called molybdomancy, was a by-product of the alchemists' attempts to transmute these base metals into gold.

A safer alternative to lead is wax. In ceromancy, melted wax is allowed to drip into a shallow dish of cold water, and the resulting shapes are interpreted. Ceromancy was very popular in the 18th century, when correspondence was normally fastened with sealing wax. And it is still important to Voodoo priests, who conduct ceromantic readings that can last from dusk to dawn.

READING COFFEE GROUNDS

You can prepare coffee grounds for a reading in the same way as you prepare tea-leaves – drinking nearly all of a cup of unstrained coffee, swirling the cup, and inverting it into the saucer. Alternatively, you can pour the dregs from your coffee cup onto a clean white plate, swirling the plate clockwise so that the liquid runs off the edge and the grounds disperse over the surface in a scattering of symbols. The recognition and interpretation of the symbols is as for tea-leaves.

READING THE TEACUPS

Positions in the cup

a Present or near future.
b More distant time.
c Unlucky area.
d The querant.
e Something departing.
f Something approaching.

Teacups used for tasseography should have a wide
mouth and sloping sides. The inner surface should be
smooth and undecorated, and be either white or a plain
pastel colour. The tea should have a fairly large leaf
and very little dust, and the cup should be filled
without using a strainer.

It is thought to be important that the querant (the
person whose fortune is to be told) actually drinks the
cup of tea, leaving just enough liquid at the bottom of
the cup to allow the leaves to be swirled. Traditionally,
the querant then takes the handle of the cup in the left
hand, and swirls the leaves clockwise, three times,
making sure that the liquid remaining in the cup
reaches right up to the rim. The querant then inverts the
cup in the saucer, and allows the liquid to drain away
for a count of seven.

You can now turn the cup the right way up, hold it with
the handle facing you, and begin the reading. You
should first consider the overall appearance of the cup:
a great many leaves implies a rich, full life; a small
scattering of a few leaves implies a tidy, disciplined
mind. Consider also the type of symbol that
predominates so that you can make an overall
assessment of good or ill fortune. Then continue with a
detailed reading of the symbols themselves.

The handle of the cup represents the querant: symbols
occurring close to the handle suggest something
occurring close to the querant's home. Symbols
pointing towards the handle imply something
approaching; those pointing away imply departure.
Some readers consider that events in the past are shown
by symbols on the left of the handle, while those in the

future are shown on the right. But more commonly the
vertical position in the cup is taken as an indication of
time, with events occurring in the present or in the near
future being shown near the rim of the cup, and those
occurring at a more distant time appearing near the
bottom. The actual bottom of the cup is considered
unlucky and indicates ill fortune.

Remember to take into account the sizes, proportions,
positions and clarity of the symbols relative to one
another. It is the overall combination of the signs that is
important: signs should not be considered in isolation.
As with so many other forms of fortune-telling, your
reading must interpret the whole picture, not just its
separate sections.

Do not worry if at first you find the symbols indistinct,
and have difficulty identifying them. It is said that if
you allow your mind to range freely, and let your
instincts and imagination take over, you will find that
practice and experience soon increase your levels of
perception.

1 Aircraft.	**7** Candle.
2 Anchor.	**8** Chair.
3 Ant.	**9** Claw.
4 Baby.	**10** Dagger.
5 Bee.	**11** Devil.
6 Bull.	**12** Dog.

EXAMPLES OF TEA-LEAF SYMBOLS

Acorn Success. At top of cup – financial success; near middle of cup – good health; near bottom of cup – improvement in health or finances.

Aircraft Sudden journey, not without risk. Can imply disappointment. If broken – an accident.

Alligator Treachery, an accident.

Anchor At top of cup – success in business and romance; middle of cup – prosperous voyage; bottom of cup – social success; obscured – anticipate difficulties.

Angel Good news.

Ant Success through perseverence.

Apple Business achievement.

Baby A series of small worries.

Ball A person connected with sport, or variable fortunes in your life.

Balloon Short-term troubles.

Beans Poverty.

Bear Facing handle – irrational decisions cause difficulties; facing away from handle – a journey.

Bee Social success, good news. Near handle of cup – friends gathering; swarm of bees – success with an audience.

Beetle Scandal, a difficult undertaking.

Bell Unexpected news. Near top of cup – promotion; near bottom of cup – sad news; two bells – joy; several bells – a wedding.

Cage A proposal.

Candle Help from others, pursuit of knowledge.

Cap Trouble ahead – be careful.

Car Good fortune.

Castle Financial gain through marriage, a strong character rising to prominence.

Cat A quarrel, treachery, a false friend.

Chain An engagement or wedding.

Chair An unexpected guest. Surrounded by dots – financial improvements.

Cherries A happy love affair.

Church Ceremony, unexpected money.

Circle Success, a wedding. With a dot – a baby; with small lines nearby – efforts hampered.

Claw A hidden enemy.

Dagger Impetuousness, danger ahead, enemies plotting.

Desk Letter containing good news.

Devil Evil influences.

Dog Good friends. If running – good news, happy meetings; at bottom of cup – friend in trouble.

Eagle A change for the better.

Ear Unexpected news.

Earrings Misunderstanding.

Easel Artistic success.

Egg Prosperity, success – the more eggs the better.

Face One face – a change, a setback; several faces – a party.

Fish Good fortune in all things, health, wealth and happiness.

Flag Danger ahead.

Fly Domestic irritations. The more flies, the more petty problems.

Frog Success through a change of home or job, avoid self-importance.

Fruit Prosperity.

Gate Opportunity, future happiness.

Goat Enemies threaten, news from a sailor.

Greyhound Good fortune.

Hand Friendship.

Harp Harmony in love.

Heart Love and marriage, a trustworthy friend.

Heather Good fortune.

Holly An important occurrence in the winter.
Horseshoe Good luck.
House Security.
Iceberg Danger.
Inkspot A letter.
Jug Gaining in importance, good health.
Key New opportunities, doors opening. Crossed keys – success; two keys near bottom of cup – robbery.
Kite Wishes coming true, do not take chances, scandal.
Knife Broken relationships. Near handle of cup – divorce; on bottom of cup – lawsuits; crossed knives – arguments.
Ladder Promotion.
Leaf Prosperity, good fortune.
Letter News. Near dots – news about money.
Lines Straight and clear – progress, journeys; wavy – uncertainty, disappointment; slanting – business failure.
Man Near handle of cup – a visitor; clear and distinct – dark-haired visitor; not well-defined – a faired-haired visitor; with arm outstretched – bringing gifts.
Moon Full – a love affair; first quarter – new projects; last quarter – fortune declining; obscured – depression; surrounded by dots – marriage for money.
Music Good fortune.
Necklace Complete – admirers; broken – the end of a relationship.
Needle Admiration.
Oak Good fortune.
Owl Gossip, scandal, failure. At bottom of cup – financial failure; near handle – domestic failure.
Parrot A scandal, a journey.
Pear Comfort, financial ease.

Purse Profit. At bottom of cup – loss.

Question mark Hesitancy, caution.

Rat Treachery.

Ring Completion. Near top of cup – marriage; near middle of cup – proposal; near bottom of cup – long engagement; complete ring – happy marriage; broken ring, or ring with cross next to it – broken engagement; two rings – plans working out.

Rose Popularity.

Scissors Domestic arguments, separation.

Shoe A change for the better.

Skeleton Loss of money, ill health.

Spider Determined and persistent, secretive, money coming.

Spoon Generosity.

Sun Happiness, success, power.

Teapot Committee meeting.

Tree Changes for the better, ambitions fulfilled. Surrounded by dots – your fortune lies in the country.

Triangle Something unexpected. Point upward – brings success; point downward – brings failure.

Umbrella Annoyances, a need for shelter. If open – shelter found; if shut – shelter refused.

Vase A friend in need.

Wheel Complete – good fortune, earned success; broken – disappointment; near rim of cup – unexpected money.

Window Open – good luck through a friend; closed – disappointment through a friend.

Wreath Happiness ahead.

Astrology

Astrology explores the effect of the sun, moon and
eight of the planets of the solar system upon the earth
and its inhabitants. It is a convention in astrology to
refer to the sun and the moon as planets, and to view
the universe as if the earth were at its centre. Thus
there are ten astrological planets that appear to move
around the earth – *planet* comes from the Greek
planets, meaning wanderer.

Each of these planets is reputed to influence our lives.
How this happens is said to be determined by the signs
of the zodiac – 12 constellations of stars beyond our
solar system that became associated with ancient
legends and myth. It was against the background of
these zodiac constellations that the planetary positions
were charted to determine the nature of events on
earth.

The horoscope or birth chart is a symbolic map of the
sky made to show the potential and characteristics of a
person born at a particular time and place on earth. A
modern birth chart is very similar in shape and form to
the charts drawn by the Greeks during the 1st and 2nd
centuries AD – the word horoscope comes from two
Greek words, *horos* meaning time, and *skopos* meaning
observer. The Greeks were also responsible for the
introduction of astrology into India and, later, into the
Arab world.

Although the Greeks did much to further the spread of
astrology, people had begun to look to the stars for
guidance very much earlier, as long ago as 8000BC.

Believing that their fates were determined from the sky, the Assyrians, Babylonians, Egyptians and Mayans all employed astrologers to observe, record and predict the positions of the stars and the timing of events important to their survival and prosperity. The first known textbook on astrology was written by the mathematician Ptolemy, who was working in Egypt between 150 and 180AD. The Greeks constructed the earliest known ephemeris (a table that shows the positions of all the planets for each day of the year). An ephemeris is similar to the nautical almanacs used by sailors to chart their positions at sea.

Astrology and Astronomy

Until the 17th century astrology, the understanding of the significance of the stars, was considered synonymous with astronomy, the study of the movements and positions of the stars. Research into astrology declined in the 18th and 19th centuries but has attracted interest again more recently, with some studies seeming to support astrological theories and others to condemn them.

Modern astrology deals with the effects that the planets are believed to have on individual lives and events, and is more often used to assess character and potential than to predict specific future events. The aim of a chart interpretation is to describe clearly the personality that is revealed in the birth chart; the traditional body of knowledge used by astrologers to do this comes from ancient mythology, centuries of observation and adaptation, and now includes ideas from analytical psychology. The calculations that are needed to make a chart of the positions of the planets for any specific time are based on astronomical information. Several methods of calculation are practiced by astrologers: here tropical astrology is used, giving the position of planets by zodiac sign.

Celestial pictures

1 Mayan calendar stone.

2 The celestial sphere according to Ptolemy's astrology, as shown in a 16th-century woodcut.

3 Early Arab zodiac.

4 Cabalistic map of the heavens, showing the stars as Hebrew letters. The Cabalists combined these letters into statements that predicted the future.

5 17th-century zodiac combining Roman, Greek and Egyptian astrology.

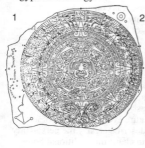

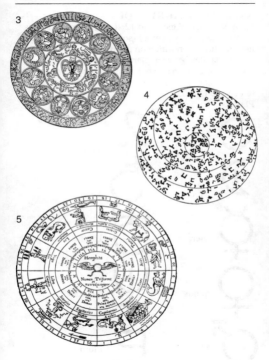

ASTROLOGICAL SYMBOLS

Each of the ten planets and 12 signs of the zodiac has its own identifying symbol (sometimes called a glyph) used to show its position on a birth chart. Some specific angles between planets (called 'aspects') are also identified by a symbol. These symbols are among the conventions of astrology with which you will need to become familiar.

Planets

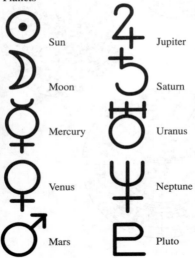

Sun

Moon

Mercury

Venus

Mars

Jupiter

Saturn

Uranus

Neptune

Pluto

Zodiac signs

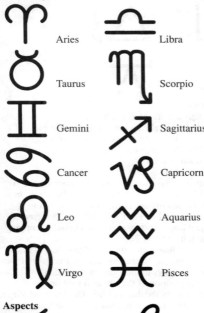

Aries

Taurus

Gemini

Cancer

Leo

Virgo

Libra

Scorpio

Sagittarius

Capricorn

Aquarius

Pisces

Aspects

Conjunction

Opposition

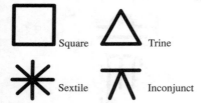

Square   Trine

Sextile   Inconjunct

Birth charts

A birth chart and its interpretation contain a great many features. Here we take an overall look at the parts of a sample chart, and at the terms in which astrologers refer to them, before going on to consider each separate feature in detail.

Parts of the chart

The complete chart shows the relative positions of 10 planets, 12 houses and 12 zodiac signs. The circle in the centre represents the earth, surrounded by the houses numbered 1 to 12. This chart has been erected by the equal house system, with each house occupying 30° of the full circle of 360°.

The horizontal line across the left of the chart is called the cusp (beginning) of the first house. The cusp of the first house is always in the ascendant position (ASC). This was the position of the sun as it rose on the eastern horizon on the date of birth. On this chart Virgo is the ascending sign, sometimes called the rising sign. The 12 signs of the zodiac are always arranged in the same order around the outer wheel but the placing of the wheel is determined by the sign of the ascendant.

Each zodiac sign occupies 30° of the outer wheel.
The positions of the planets are marked on the inner
edge of the zodiac wheel and are identified by their
symbols. MC stands for the Latin *medium coeli*
meaning midheaven. The midheaven is on the cusp of
the tenth house indicating the position of the sun at noon
on the date of birth. If the clock time of birth is not
known, the sun can be placed in the midheaven
position and the houses omitted.

Unlike geographical maps, south is always placed at
the top of a birth chart. Consequently the sun-sign of
a person born during the day will be in the upper half
of the chart; for a person born during the night, the
sun-sign will be in the lower half of the chart. Ms S was
born in the early afternoon, so her sun-sign Gemini is in
the upper half.

A sample birth chart

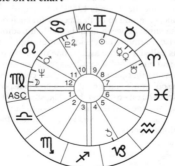

This is the birth chart of Ms S, who was born on May 25, 1931: her date of birth is used to find the positions of the planets when it is noon at Greenwich, England on that date. Ms S was born at 2.30pm BST. As the time given is British Summer Time (BST) it must be corrected to Greenwich Mean Time (GMT) in order to calculate the chart. The corrected time is 1.30pm GMT. The latitude and longitude of the place of birth are also used in the calculations. Ms S was born near Preston in England, located 53°46' north of the equator and 2°41' west of the Greenwich meridian.

Table of major aspects

This table, containing information extracted from the birth chart, shows the precise positions of the planets in degrees and minutes. Measurements around the zodiac wheel are made counterclockwise, so it can be seen, for example, that the sun on the chart is only 3°22' into Gemini, while the moon is 13°11' into Virgo.

The planets are said to be in aspect with each other when the angle between them is one that traditionally emphasises harmony or tension. For example, an angle of 90° is called a square aspect; one of 120° a trine aspect; and one of 60° a sextile aspect. The sun's aspects with other planets on this chart can be read from the column headed by the sun on the aspect table. Each aspect has its own symbol. The sun is square Neptune: an aspect of tension. The moon, however, is trine Mercury and Venus, and sextile Jupiter: these are harmonious aspects.

Position of planet	☉	☽	☿	♀	♂	♃	♄	♅	♆	Planet
3°22' ♊										☉ Sun
13°11' ♍										☽ Moon
8°52' ♉		△								☿ Mercury
5°22' ♉		△	☌							♀ Venus
21°45' ♌										♂ Mars
18°59' ♋		✳								♃ Jupiter
22°54' ♑					✳	☍				♄ Saturn
17°56' ♈					△	□	□			♅ Uranus
3°2' ♍	□		△	△						♆ Neptune
19°15' ♋						☌	☍	□		♇ Pluto

ASC	24°30' ♍
MC	24°30' ♊

1 Qualities and elements associated with zodiac signs

Table 1 shows the three qualities, sometimes called the triplicities, and the four elements, sometimes known as the quadruplicities, which combined together represent the 12 zodiac signs. The planets are placed in the box appropriate to the zodiac sign in which they are situated on the chart.

It can be seen that there are five planets in earth signs on this chart, and that the planets are fairly evenly distributed among the three qualities. Thus the astrological signature of this chart is balanced earth.

1

Qualities	Elements Fire	Earth	Air	Water
Cardinal	♅	♄		♇ ♃
Fixed	♂	☿ ♀		
Mutable		☽ ♆		☉

2 Qualities and areas of interest associated with houses

Table 2 relates to the houses in which the planets are situated. Three qualities, similar to those associated with the zodiac signs but with different names, are combined with four areas of interest to produce 12 houses.

It can be seen that five planets are in houses of completion on this chart and that the planets are once more fairly evenly spread across the three house qualities, indicating that Ms S's main interest in life is in making balanced endings.

2

Qualities	Areas of interest Life	Purpose	Relationship	Endings
Angular		♇ ♃	♅	♄
Succedent			♂	☿ ♀
Cadent	☉			☽ ♆

3

a Mutual reception	None
b Dignity	♄ in ♑ ♀ in ♉
c Detriment	♆ in ♍
d Exaltation	♃ in ♋
e Fall	None
f Ascendant ruler	☿
g Dispositor	♀
h Rising planets	None
i Chart shape	Bucket

3 Other features of the chart

An astrologer may also extract a number of other significant features from a chart: some of these are shown in Table 3.

a When two planets are placed in each other's sign, they are said to be in mutual reception. Each planet traditionally rules one or two of the zodiac signs. For example, the sun is the natural ruler of Leo and the moon of Cancer, so if the sun is in Cancer and the moon in Leo, the sun and moon would be in mutual reception, a very harmonious arrangement. There are no planets in mutual reception in this chart.

b Planets are in dignity when they are in the sign of which they are the natural ruler. Saturn rules Capricorn and Venus rules Taurus, so Saturn and Venus are both in dignity in this chart, powerful and fortunate positions.

c Detriment is the opposite to dignity and happens when a planet is in the sign opposite to the one it would naturally rule. Neptune is the natural ruler of Pisces, but in this chart Neptune is placed in the opposite sign of Virgo; Neptune in Virgo is in a detrimental position.

d Planets are exalted when they are in the sign from which they draw the source of their power. Jupiter in this chart is exalted in Cancer.

e Other signs are said to restrict a planet's power: the planet is then said to be in fall. For example, if Jupiter were in Capricorn, the sign of law and limitations, Jupiter's expansive power would be restricted. There are no planets in fall on this chart.

f The planet that is the natural ruler of the sign on the ascendant is called the ascendant ruler; in this chart it is Mercury, because Mercury rules Virgo. Mercury also rules Gemini (the sun-sign on this chart), which makes Mercury doubly important.

g A planet is said to be the dispositor when it disposes of or takes over the rulership of the whole chart. Taking each planet on the chart in turn, the rulership of the sign in which it is placed is followed through to conclusion.

The sun is in Gemini. Gemini is ruled by Mercury. Mercury on the chart is in Taurus. Taurus is ruled by Venus. Venus on the chart is in Taurus, and Venus rules Taurus, so Venus is said to dispose of Mercury, rather like a take-over bid.

The same conclusion is reached for all the planets, making Venus the dispositor of all other rulers on this chart. Since Venus is already in dignity in Taurus, this makes Venus very important.

h Rising planets are those that are placed on or very close to the ascendant. No planet is close enough to the ascendant in this chart to be called a rising planet and thus gain the extra importance such a planet is given.

i The shape of a chart is determined from the pattern made by the planets. This is a bucket chart, with the planets in the upper half forming the base of the bucket and the single planet, Saturn, alone in the lower half forming the handle. As Saturn is also in dignity in Capricorn, Saturn would be given special attention in the interpretation of this chart.

CHARACTERISTICS

Before a birth chart can be fully comprehended, the characteristics of the planets, zodiac signs and houses must first be understood. As their separate meanings become clear, so the links between them will fall into place.

The tables for the zodiac signs and the houses can be read together, as the order given links the signs across the table with their natural houses. For example, the first house has many Arien characteristics, the second house many Taurean characteristics and so on. There is also a natural progression downward through the table of houses.

As it is a convention of astrology to call the sun and moon planets, ten planets appear on a birth chart. Each zodiac sign is ruled by the planet that is most in

harmony with it temperamentally. Venus, for example,
is in harmony with Taurean loyalty and with a Libran
need to be fair-minded: thus Venus rules both Taurus
and Libra.

CUSPS

The cusp of a sign or a house marks its starting point.
The cusps of the signs and houses do not usually
coincide, as can be seen in Ms S's chart. The cusps of
the first, fourth, seventh and tenth houses – the angular
houses – are particularly important, and are indicated
on the chart by double lines.

Planets on the cusp of a sign are just entering the
named sign, and so the personality may retain some of
the characteristics of the previous sign.

THE PLANETS
What?
This is the question answered by the position of a planet in a chart. For example, you would find out what changes might be likely by locating the position of Uranus on the chart.

	Planet	Symbolism	Area of Influence
☉	Sun	Source of life	Personality
☽	Moon	Mirror of life	Moods
☿	Mercury	Messenger	Thoughts
♀	Venus	Goddess of love	Feelings and values
♂	Mars	Warrior	Action and drive
♃	Jupiter	Prophet	Expansion
♄	Saturn	Lawgiver	Responsibilities
♅	Uranus	Awakener	Changes
♆	Neptune	Mystic	Imagination
♇	Pluto	Dark lord	Transformation

A brief interpretation of the planets
The sun Energising and fortifying, the sun is the masculine principle in everyone's makeup. Associated with dignity, health, leadership, ego and the capacity for experience.

The moon Nurturing and receptive, the moon is the feminine principle in everyone's makeup. Associated with fluctuations, cycles, habits, reflex actions, desires, fertility and the need to touch.

Mercury Quick and versatile, Mercury influences reason, thought, the capacity for emotion, local travel and activities, dexterity, words and the intellect, and everything associated with communication.

Venus Gentle and sensuous, Venus influences love, the arts, affections, pleasures, possessions, morality, marriage, sociability and whatever is most valued.

Mars Active and competitive, Mars is linked with power, physical movement, construction, sexual energy, courage, self-assertion, strength and initiative.

Jupiter Broad-minded Jupiter aspires to philosophy, benevolence, prosperity, optimism, growth and long-distance travel. He likes to have plenty of space.

Saturn Persistent and wise, Saturn is associated with truth, aging, ambition, responsibility, the capacity for a career and with all the great lessons life can teach us. Saturn's placing in the chart may indicate restrictive overcompensation against feelings of insecurity.

Uranus Original and humanitarian Uranus is the breaker of traditions, associated with science, invention, magic, electricity, psychology, the will and the unexpected.

Neptune Subtle and mysterious, Neptune rules the sea, all liquids, illusions, dreams, deceptions, ideals, religions, and thus rules drama, films, anaesthetics, drugs, prisons, hospitals and all institutions.

Pluto Ruler of the underworld, Pluto reveals what has been hidden including the subconscious self. Pluto rules atomic power, birth and death, group processes and problem areas we have to solve alone and unaided.

THE SIGNS OF THE ZODIAC
How?

This is the question answered by the signs of the zodiac. For example, you can discover how a person thinks by locating the sign in which Mercury is placed. (Mercury's area of influence is the thoughts.)

	Zodiac sign	Name	Quality	Element	Ruler
♈	Aries	Ram	Cardinal	Fire	Mars
♉	Taurus	Bull	Fixed	Earth	Venus
♊	Gemini	Twins	Mutable	Air	Mercury
♋	Cancer	Crab	Cardinal	Water	Moon
♌	Leo	Lion	Fixed	Fire	Sun
♍	Virgo	Virgin	Mutable	Earth	Mercury
♎	Libra	Scales	Cardinal	Air	Venus
♏	Scorpio	Scorpion	Fixed	Water	Pluto
♐	Sagittarius	Archer	Mutable	Fire	Jupiter
♑	Capricorn	Goat	Cardinal	Earth	Saturn
♒	Aquarius	Waterman	Fixed	Air	Uranus
♓	Pisces	Fishes	Mutable	Water	Neptune

The three qualities of the signs

Cardinal signs use their abilities to achieve ambitions.
Fixed signs hold on to what they have and resist change.
Mutable signs are always searching and often changing.

The four elements

Fire Glowing or volcanic, fire is not easy to contain and is a process, not a substance. Once burning, fire will use up air and may boil water or scorch earth.

Earth Solid or sandy, earth can be used for building or planting; it can channel water, make a fireplace and coexist with air.

Air Windy or balmy, air is always on the move and quite invisible; it rises above earth, makes bubbles in water and is transformed by fire to which it is essential.

Water Clear or muddy, water seeks its own level and can evaporate, freeze and reflect rainbows; it can put out a fire, flood the earth and dampen air. By further considering how fire, earth, air and water behave you can extend your interpretation of the signs.

The duality of the zodiac qualities and elements

Combining the qualities and elements of the signs gives an indication of characteristic behaviour. As we all choose how to behave, these characteristics can be positive – or negative.

Aries Independent, dynamic – arrogant, hasty.

Taurus Loyal, stable – possessive, stubborn.

Gemini Adaptable, communicative – scheming, gossipy.

Cancer Sympathetic, sensitive – manipulative, touchy.

Leo Self-assured, generous – pompous, pretentious.

Virgo Discriminating, humane – petty, insular.

Libra Refined, diplomatic – apathetic, fickle.

Scorpio Probing, passionate – suspicious, jealous.

Sagittarius Enthusiastic, honest – big-headed, blunt.

Capricorn Responsible, economical – inhibited, mean.

Aquarius Altruistic, just – vague, two-faced.

Pisces Sacrificing, intuitive – lazy, unreliable.

THE HOUSES

Where?

This is the question answered by the houses. For example, you can discover where most energy will be expended by locating the house in which Mars is placed. (Mars' area of interest is action and drive.)

The three qualities of the houses

Angular houses are where action is initiated.

Succedent houses are where action is stabilised.

Cadent houses are where we learn from actions and adapt.

	Quality	Element	Areas of everyday life
1	Angular	Life	Identity and outlook
2	Succedent	Purpose	Values and freedom
3	Cadent	Relationships	Awareness and contact
4	Angular	Endings	Security and home
5	Succedent	Life	Creativity and children
6	Cadent	Purpose	Work and service
7	Angular	Relationships	Marriage and partnership
8	Succedent	Endings	Regeneration and sex
9	Cadent	Life	Aspiration and beliefs
10	Angular	Purpose	Honour and status
11	Succedent	Relationships	Friends and hopes
12	Cadent	Endings	Subconscious secrets

The four house elements

The houses of life People with several planets in these houses have boundless energy, enthusiasm and conviction. *First house*: physical energy. *Fifth house*: creative energy. *Ninth house*: spiritual energy.

The houses of purpose People with several planets in these houses are stable, reliable and practical. *Second house*: possessions and finances. *Sixth house*: occupation. *Tenth house*: recognition.

The houses of relationships People with several planets in these houses need other people. *Third house*: chance relationships. *Seventh house*: close relationships. *Eleventh house*: social relationships.

The houses of endings People with several planets in these houses are sensitive to the way in which we may attain freedom. *Fourth house*: letting go of physical security. *Eighth house*: enlightenment of the mind.

Twelfth house: release from secret fears.

The cusps of the angular houses These are particularly important points on a chart.

Cusp of the first house of life This is the ascendant; your appearance in the world and how other people often see you on first acquaintance.

Cusp of the fourth house of endings This is the point of origin; your family roots and psychological foundation.

Cusp of the seventh house of relationships This is the descendant (where the sun set on the day of your birth); here you relate with another and begin to lose yourself.

Cusp of the tenth house of purpose This is the MC or midheaven; the high point of achievement and what has been learned from life.

INTRODUCTION

Understanding a chart can be compared to getting to know a new piece of music. You first gain a general impression; then, as the chart is read in detail, the main themes emerge to be followed by the more subtle connections.

The first impression is made by the shape of the chart – the general pattern made by the arrangement of the planets. Seven major shapes can be distinguished, and these are said to coincide with the seven major personality types. The shapes can be a useful guide when you are interpreting a chart, and may also give extra emphasis to a characteristic that appears in your more detailed interpretation.

As it is the placing of the planets in the zodiac signs that is significant in deciding the shape of a chart, here we show the seven major types of charts without house divisions.

Similarly, the individual names of the planets are not needed when forming this general impression, and so their positions are indicated by dots.

THE SEVEN MAJOR CHART SHAPES

1 Splash In this type of chart the planets occupy as many signs as possible, and may be spread fairly evenly around the wheel. At their best, splash people have wide interests – but at their worst may spread themselves too thinly.

2 Bundle Here the planets are grouped closely together in four or five consecutive signs. This is the rarest of the major chart shapes, and indicates a personality with a driving specialist interest.

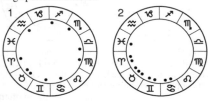

3 Locomotive The planets in this type of chart are generally arranged fairly evenly around nine consecutive signs, leaving an empty group of three signs. The name locomotive is used because in engineering a driving wheel has an extra weight of metal to create a balance against the driving rod. Locomotive people have exceptional drive and application to the task in hand. The leading planet moving clockwise around the wheel is important, as it may indicate which area of the personality is a prime motivating force.

4 Bowl This shape is easy to recognise because all the planets fall in approximately half the chart. Bowl people scoop up experience and are very self-contained; the leading planet of the bowl could be said to lead them into various experiences. The bowl has particular importance if all the planets fall above or below the horizontal line of the ascendant, or if they all fall in the eastern or western halves of the chart.

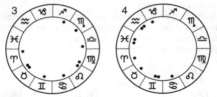

5 Bucket Here nine of the planets fall in one half of the chart, while the tenth (called the singleton) is placed opposite them, forming the handle of the bucket. Bucket people direct their energies toward the achievement of one objective, and the singleton often indicates the nature of this purpose. They are not usually very concerned with self-preservation.

6 Seesaw To form this shape of chart two groups of planets must appear opposite each other, and there must be two or more empty signs in the two empty sections. The number of planets in each group may vary, but ideally there should be five planets on each side of the chart. Seesaw people always see both sides of an issue and may view life itself from two points of view. They may need to balance their interests and activities.

7 Splay This arrangement of planets is not always easy to define, but there must be at least one group of two or three planets placed closely together while the rest are distributed around the chart. Empty signs are usually distributed evenly as well. Splay people are individualists who do not like being classified or regimented. A splay chart may have planets in all three of one of the elements. For example, planets in all three earth signs would indicate an individualist in practical affairs, while planets in all three air signs would suggest intellectual independence.

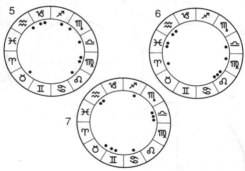

SEMICIRCLES AND QUARTERS

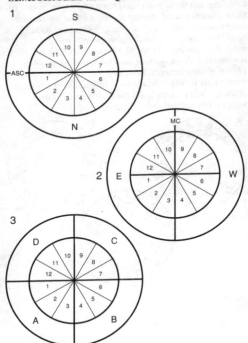

The line extending the ascendant across the centre of a chart (**1**) is called the horizon or equator. Planets appearing in houses 1-6 below this line are in the northern half of the chart and are called the night planets. Planets placed in houses 7-12 above the horizon are in the southern half of the chart and are called the day planets.

The line extending vertically down the middle of a chart from the MC (**2**) is called the meridian. Planets placed to the left of the meridian are called eastern planets; those placed to the right are called western planets. The four major semicircles of a chart are thus: day, representing objectivity and an outgoing nature; night, representing subjectivity and privacy; east, indicating free will and independence; and west, indicating flexibility and dependence.

Combining the meridian with the horizon (**3**) gives the four major quarters of a chart. Planets in houses 1-3 occupy the eastern night quarter (**A**); planets in houses 4-6 occupy the western night quarter (**B**); planets in houses 7-9 occupy the western day quarter (**C**); planets in houses 1-12 occupy the eastern day quarter (**D**). Each quarter represents a combination of the characteristics of the contributing semicircles. The eastern night quarter indicates a love of privacy and dislike of compromise; the western night quarter indicates imagination and a reserved nature; the western day quarter indicates ambition combined with a somewhat indecisive nature; and the eastern day quarter indicates a rebellious independence.

BOWL CHARTS

Bowl-shape charts in which all the planets are placed exclusively in one major half of the chart are not common, but when they occur they add extra emphasis to the bowl characteristics. They present a challenge that can be met by scooping up experience and using it to advantage. Bowl charts are named from the semicircle in which the planets fall: a day bowl chart, for example, is one in which all the planets are in the day half.

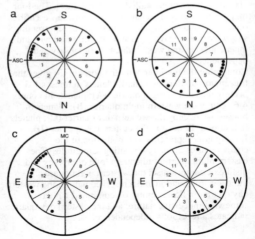

Day bowl A person with this chart is likely to be ambitious (and even somewhat calculating and self centred), with many acquaintances and a small number of very close friends. Queen Victoria (**a**) and the novelist Henry James both had day bowl charts.

Night bowl A person with this chart is probably a natural loner who is shy, but who may have unusual insights and a natural artistic talent. Night bowl charts include those of the English poets Elizabeth Barrett Browning (**b**) and John Milton, and of the Flemish painter Rubens.

East bowl A person with this chart is often very individualistic, dislikes taking orders or making compromises and may have difficulty with personal relationships. East bowl charts include those of the author Franz Kafka (**c**), the composer Stravinsky and the artist Marc Chagall.

West bowl A person with this chart can develop good human relations, is socially diplomatic, but may be strongly influenced by the opinions of others and so find self-assertion difficult. US President Woodrow Wilson (**d**) and the deaf and blind Helen Keller both had west bowl charts.

POSITIONS OF THE PLANETS

Before interpreting a chart an astrologer will read the positions of the planets in order, noting them down so that there are no omissions. The positions of the sun, moon and ascendant are usually noted at the top of a reading, because these are the three most important placements.

A table of dignities gives more information about the rulership of the planets. Information from this table is also noted down as it is essential for a complete reading.

TABLE OF DIGNITIES

Dignity If you have a planet in dignity, you control the conditions in that part of your chart.

Detriment If you have a planet in detriment, you must accept the conditions in that part of your chart.

Exaltation If you have a planet in exaltation, you feel very positive and happy in that part of your chart.

Fall A planet in fall indicates an area of your chart where you may not feel at ease. For example, the sun is in fall in Libra. This does not mean that one-twelfth of the world's population is uncomfortable! It means that people with the Libran sun sign are always trying to improve their circumstances, and have an urge to try and keep everything around them harmonious.

Conventions of rulership Before the discovery of Uranus, Neptune and Pluto – the planets that now rule Aquarius, Pisces and Scorpio respectively – these three zodiac signs had other ruling planets, often called the old rulers. The old ruler of Scorpio was Mars, the old ruler of Aquarius was Saturn and the old ruler of Pisces was Jupiter. The table of dignities takes account of the old rulership.

When the idea of rulership was first developed, Mars, Saturn and Jupiter were given dual characteristics that now match the modern interpretations given to Pluto, Uranus and Neptune. It is thought by some astrologers that there are still two more planets to be discovered in our solar system, and that these will become the rulers of Virgo and Libra. Meanwhile, Virgo is ruled by Mercury and Libra by Venus.

Planets in mutual reception

Mutual reception occurs when two planets are in one another's sign of the zodiac. Mutual reception emphasises the energies of both planets as they work together.

Plant	Dignity	Detriment	Exaltation	Fall
☉ Sun	♌	♒	♈	♎
☽ Moon	♋	♑	♉	♏
☿ Mercury	♊ ♍	♐ ♓	♍ ♒	♓
♀ Venus	♉ ♎	♏ ♈	♓	♍
♂ Mars	♈ ♏	♎ ♉	♑	♋
♃ Jupiter	♐ ♓	♊ ♍	♋	♑
♄ Saturn	♑ ♒	♋ ♌	♎	♈
♅ Uranus	♒	♌	♏	♉
♆ Neptune	♓	♍	♋	♑
♇ Pluto	♏	♉	♓	♍

SUN SIGN TABLES

This diagram (**A**) will allow most people to find their sun sign easily. However, the sun does enter and leave signs on slightly different dates in some years. So anyone born on or near the cusp of a sign will need to check further in a detailed table of sun sign changes – one of the reference works you will need when you begin to draw up detailed charts. For example, an extract (**B**) from such a table for 1953 shows that the sun entered Aquarius on January 20 at 8.22 hours GMT, entered Pisces on February 18 at 22.41 hours GMT and so on.

A

Aries
March 22 – April 20

Taurus
April 21 – May 21

Gemini
May 22 – June 22

Cancer
June 23 – July 23

Leo
July 24 – August 23

Virgo
August 24 – September 23

♎ **Libra**
September 24 – October 23

♏ **Scorpio**
October 24 – November 22

♐ **Sagittarius**
November 23 – December 22

♑ **Capricorn**
December 23 – January 19

♒ **Aquarius**
January 20 – February 19

♓ **Pisces**
February 20 – March 21

B

	20 ♒ 8.22	18 ♓ 22.41	20 ♈ 22.01	20 ♉ 9.26	21 ♊ 8.53	21 ♋ 17.00
	1	2	3	4	5	6

23 ♌ 3.53	23 ♍ 10.46	23 ♎ 8.07	23 ♏ 17.07	22 ♐ 14.23	22 ♑ 3.32
7	8	9	10	11	12

INTERPRETATIONS OF PLANETS IN ZODIAC SIGNS AND HOUSES

An astrologer who has prepared a complete reading from a client's birth chart then goes on to consider the interpretations of the ten planets in the different zodiac signs and houses. Here we consider them in their traditional order of importance, beginning with the sun. The positions of the sun, the moon and the ascendant symbolise a person's essential nature, and are often related to the past, present and future parts of a life cycle. The sun expresses personality in the present, the moon reflects moods to which we have become conditioned in the past, and the ascendant represents the future outlook. The ascendant in a sign shares the same potentials as the sun in that sign, and so the same interpretations apply.

During the earlier part of life the sun and moon are said to dominate the chart as the sun seeks to express itself and come to terms with the moon's influence. Yet underlying the whole chart is the subtle influence of the ascendant that symbolises the leader of the succession of signs and houses around the chart, and orients them in time and space.

The ascendant is always on the cusp of the first house of self, but may be in any one of the zodiac signs. It symbolises the outlook of the person, and influences physical appearance. In astrological terms, maturity is said to be reached when the person has begun to express the nature of the outlook represented by the ascendant sign. The mature self is said to emerge as the parts of the personality (in particular those represented by the sun and the moon) are integrated and the individual achieves full expression.

The sun, the moon, Mercury, Venus and Mars are regarded as the personal planets, symbolising individual resources. They move quite quickly through the signs, ranging from the moon, which stays in a sign for only about two days before moving on, to Mars, which may stay for about two months. Although slower-moving, Jupiter and Saturn also modify the personality. Jupiter takes about a year to move through a sign, and Saturn about 2 ¹/₂ years.

The planets that move very slowly – Uranus, Neptune and Pluto – are regarded as the generation planets representing collective resources. The signs in which these planets are placed on a chart show how people born within a few years of each other are likely to respond to the larger social issues. The aspects made by these planets and their house positions are more important in a chart than their sign position. Uranus takes about seven years to move through a sign; Neptune takes about 14 years; and Pluto takes 13-32 years.

The separate interpretations for the positions of the planets in the signs and houses should never stand alone – they should always be considered in relation to each other. The aspects between the planets should also be taken into account, as should the natural house positions and planetary rulers of the signs. No single feature of a birth chart should be considered in isolation: seeing the whole picture is the real art of interpretation.

Traditional planets

Until the 18th century, astrological treatises described and illustrated the influence of only seven planets, as shown in the woodcut. The seven 'traditional' planets – the sun, the moon, Mercury, Venus, Mars, Jupiter and Saturn – are all visible to the naked eye, and have probably been known since prehistoric times. The so-called 'modern' planets can only be seen with a telescope: Uranus was discovered in 1781, Neptune in 1846 and Pluto in 1930.

SUN
Symbolism Source of life.
Area of influence Personality.
Associated with dignity, health, ego and leadership; the sun's place in the chart shows how and where you want to shine.

The sun in the zodiac signs

Aries Headstrong, enterprising, you like to do your own thing and have your own way; may be opinionated.

Taurus Persistent, steadfast, you like luxury and security; a faithful friend but an implacable enemy.

Gemini Sensitive, restless, eloquent, you love variety and change and like to socialise; may be vague.

Cancer Cautious, broody, imaginative, you like to feel secure. Home is important; defensive when shy.

Leo Confident, proud, generous, you stand up for yourself; you like attention and can be patronising.

Virgo Modest, cool-headed, thoughtful, you have a strong sense of duty; may be fussy about rules.

Libra Charming, sociable, diplomatic, you are always able to compromise with others; may be indecisive.

Scorpio Determined, shrewd, secretive, you like to know all that is going on; can be jealous and sharp.

Sagittarius Friendly, enthusiastic, tolerant, you love freedom and adventure; may be extravagant and blunt.

Capricorn Self-disciplined, loyal, serious, practical, you work hard to achieve; sometimes slow to trust others.

Aquarius Unpredictable, full of new ideas, you like to express your ideas freely; can be rebellious and distant.

Pisces Versatile, sensitive, kind to others, you love to dream but may sometimes find it hard to be practical.

The sun in the houses

1 Here the sun acquires some Arien characteristics and is strongly placed. Personal affairs need much time.

2 Here the sun acts like a Taurean sun. Ambition for material gains and effective at acquiring things.

3 The sun here has many of the communicative qualities of Gemini. A lively mind, friendly to neighbours.

4 Often conservative and strongly influenced by home. Here the sun shows Cancerian qualities.

5 Here the sun behaves like Leo, the sign it rules. A strong place for creativity, success and enjoyment.

6 Dedicated to good work habits and health, keen to help others. The sun here acts like the sun in Virgo.

7 Friends and enemies are the key to the personality with the sun here, behaving much like a Libran sun.

8 Here the sun has many Scorpionic qualities. Has a deep interest in the nature of things.

9 Here the sun has some Sagittarian characteristics. High ideals, broad interests, perhaps foreign travel.

10 Here the sun takes on some qualities of Capricorn and gains purpose and a desire for status and success.

11 Social ambition and cooperative ventures appeal to the sun placed here, behaving much like an Aquarian.

12 Here the sun may have difficulty expressing itself fully, acquiring the dreaminess of a Piscean sun.

MOON
Symbolism Mirror of life.
Area of influence Moods.
Associated with emotions, devotion and the nurturing instinct; the moon's place in the chart reflects your moods.

The moon in the zodiac signs
Aries Emotionally dominating but can blow hot or cold. Sincere, enthusiastic, but nervous at asking for help.

Taurus Emotionally steady, can be loyal or stubborn. Faithful, sentimental, affectionate, but may be timid.

Gemini Emotionally versatile, perceptive, often able to be dispassionate; may need to do several things at once.

Cancer Emotionally possessive but can be totally devoted and trusting. Thrifty, intuitive, easily hurt.

Leo Emotionally bountiful but can be fiery and self-concerned. Magnetic, romantic, honest and loving.

Virgo Emotionally appreciative but can seem very shy. Generous but emotionally demanding and insecure.

Libra Emotionally gracious but needs to be approved of by others. Sociable, affectionate but indecisive.

Scorpio Emotionally intense but often very controlled. Can be jealous, proud, sacrificial, but deeply hurt.

Sagittarius Emotionally idealistic, acute judgement, but a happy-go-lucky naivety and a need for total freedom.

Capricorn Emotionally inhibited but supersensitive and dignified. Can be melancholic or have rare great passions.

Aquarius Emotionally detached, a preference for cool friendship. Very idealistic but needs outlets for tension.

Pisces Emotionally subjective with an instinctive feeling for others. Sometimes sentimental and self-pitying.

The moon in the houses

1 Very imaginative and sensitive to feelings within the self. Moody and changeable, perhaps shy.

2 Capable of being very persuasive, has a great need for material security. Can be generous or mean.

3 Restless, expressive, dramatic. A lack of long-term concentration, but a good memory and avid curiosity.

4 A very strong feeling for home, family, parents or family history, although there may be many changes.

5 Strong romantic emotions and a love of theatrical effects. Creative in cycles. Often fond of children.

6 A strong desire to serve or look after people. Rather nervous, changeable in habits. Has vague illnesses.

7 Responsive to others' needs and generally popular, but indecisive. Subject to changes in friendships.

8 A great need for security and thus an interest in love, sex and affection. Can sometimes be rather morbid.

9 Very philosophical with a natural ability to teach others. Likes to study the meaning of life at any level.

10 Sometimes this position is like living on constant view to the public. May be many changes of occupation.

11 An objective view of organisations and clubs. Often many helpful friends; sometimes some false friends.

12 Rather retiring and uncomfortable in strange surroundings. Often likes seclusion or working alone.

MERCURY
Symbolism The messenger.
Area of influence Thoughts, mind.
Associated with reasoning ability, words, travel and dexterity; Mercury's place in the chart shows how you best communicate.

Mercury in the zodiac signs

Aries An impulsive mind, quick, direct, witty, inventive. Looks ahead, can improvise, but may be impatient.

Taurus A mind that values facts and weighs the evidence. May have mental inertia.

Gemini A very quick, communicative, logical, witty and perceptive mind. Many thoughts, may not be thorough.

Cancer A receptive, impressionable, retentive mind. Arguments make you adamant. Very subjective.

Leo Broad-minded, able to solve problems and speak with authority, may ignore details or be quick-tempered.

Virgo An analytical, practical, methodical, sensible mind. Able to be impersonal, sometimes critical.

Libra An active, diplomatic and just mind, looking for the perfect compromise. Dislikes losing arguments.

Scorpio An acute, shrewd, probing mind. Opinions rarely change and can be forcefully stated.

Sagittarius An independent, progressive, honest mind. May be scatterbrained, often very direct or even blunt.

Capricorn A serious, cautious, ambitious mind with a memory for detail. Dry-witted or even satirical.

Aquarius A resourceful, original, observant mind with an interest in abstract ideas. Can be stubborn or eccentric.

Pisces A very receptive, osmotic mind capable of exact insight; can be woolly-minded and sometimes morbid.

Mercury in the houses

1 Self-conscious, you may find it hard to understand the feelings of others. Point of view starts from the self.

2 Value-conscious with a rational, commercial sensitivity. Point of view starts from 'What can I gain'?

3 Communication-conscious and restless, you may say 'What can I learn, where can I go, who can I meet'?

4 Family-conscious and thrifty, your point of view begins from home, family, history or a need to collect.

5 Pleasure-conscious and full of bright ideas, you are on the lookout for novelty, chance, fun and lots of affairs.

6 Conscious of duty, you apply thought systematically – a need to have back-up plans and many irons in the fire.

7 People-conscious, your outlook starts from 'What can we do together'? Partnerships are important.

8 Conscious of hidden motives and intuitive, your point of view starts from 'What's really going on here'?

9 Conscious there is always something new to be learned, your outlook is free-ranging and philosophical.

10 Conscious of status, your point of view begins from 'How can these facts be used to my best advantage'?

11 Socially conscious, your thoughts are concerned with what is best for a group of people.

12 Conscious of inner feelings on which you base decisions, you may be guarded or insecure.

VENUS
Symbolism Goddess of love.
Area of influence Feelings, values.
Associated with affections,
sensuality and pleasure; the position
of Venus in the chart shows where
your values lie.

Venus in the zodiac signs

Aries Magnetic, ardent, demonstrative, outgoing, you like to present yourself well. May be overwhelming.

Taurus Faithful, steadfast, sensual, artistic, you love luxury and touching things. May be possessive.

Gemini Generous, friendly, bright, you love to roam around freely. May be fickle in romance or affection.

Cancer Idealistic, gentle, devoted, caring, you have an instinct to nurture. May become too clinging.

Leo Warm-hearted, lavish, romantic, you love life and love to be noticed. Can be very jealous.

Virgo Undemonstrative, shy, inhibited, your sensuality is hidden. Can behave in exactly the opposite way.

Libra Attractive, gracious, appreciative, you may be more in love with love than with your partner.

Scorpio Passionate, magnetic, loyal, you can feel desolate or become cruel if rejected sexually.

Sagittarius Adventurous, humourous, idealistic, you deal out affection freely but may hate commitments.

Capricorn Dedicated, proud, reserved on the surface, you may hide a fear of your sensuality being rejected.

Aquarius Detached, cool, friendly, you do not like to be tied down and may prefer platonic relationships.

Pisces Gentle, compassionate, tender, you may be very self-sacrificing or much too hypersensitive.

Venus in the houses

1 You value yourself, and are often happy, balanced and kind. You enjoy luxury and may like to be spoiled.

2 You value your possessions and talents, and like your work to be pleasant in luxurious surroundings.

3 You value pleasant friendships and a charming family. You dislike arguments and prefer persuasion to force.

4 You value a comfortable, organised home, which you may create yourself. Your ethical values are strong.

5 You value affection, pleasure and giving pleasure to others, children, love affairs and creative ventures.

6 You value service both given and received. You may be a 'Good Samaritan', if sometimes indulgently.

7 You value harmony, the law and social graces. You may be happy in marriage, business or in public life.

8 You value sensuality and life itself. Spiritual peace may be important. You may benefit greatly from others.

9 You value enthusiasm and zeal, whether you have it yourself or not, and you enjoy travel.

10 You value status and diplomacy and may be very popular with associates who are willing to help you.

11 You value a variety of friendships and affiliations, but sometimes you may be too idealistic in a group.

12 You value seclusion and privacy, from which position you may feel an urge to serve others.

MARS
Symbolism The warrior.
Area of influence Action, drive.
Associated with power, sex and
competition; Mars' position in the
chart shows how and where energy
is used.

Mars in the zodiac signs

Aries Energy used for self-willed vigorous action; a
dislike of routine or timidity. Sexually dynamic.
Taurus Energy used to plow through all obstacles; likes
to be the boss. Sexually earthy but may be jealous.
Gemini Energy used to put ideas into action quickly;
can sell anyone anything. Sexually prefers variety.
Cancer Energy used acquisitively and protectively; may
smoulder emotionally. Sexually sensitive.
Leo Energy used to act generously and courageously.
Great sex appeal – winner or loser but never also-ran.
Virgo Energy used to develop strategies for perfection;
may be more ardent in work than in love. Sexually shy.
Libra Energy used paradoxically to fight for peace.
Sexually, likes the soft lights and sweet music approach.
Scorpio Energy from vast hidden sources tends to
explode into action. Sexually demands all or nothing.
Sagittarius Energy used for a perpetual love affair with
life; sometimes burns the candle at both ends.
Capricorn Energy used to sustain effort; may speak
softly and carry a big stick. Sexually persistent.
Aquarius Energy used galvanically for break-ups,
break-downs and break-throughs. Sexually innovative.
Pisces Energy often remains inward under pressure;
dislike of physical action. Romantic and sensual.

Mars in the houses

1 Self-assertive, practical, competitive, may be boisterous. Keen to prove self.

2 Resourceful, generous. Devotes energy to getting rich quickly but may lose the gains just as quickly.

3 Assertive with words, impatient, restless, may be tactless. Loves to get into arguments or debates.

4 Devotes much energy to fulfilling a need for security. May have to move from birthplace.

5 Impulsive, a born promoter, may be athletic, likes to be up and doing but may be a bad loser. Creative.

6 Puts energy into work and service and expects others to do so too. A passion for orderliness in any area.

7 Energy attracts strong reactions one way or another from other people. May be a controversial personality.

8 Much energy devoted to lusty matters such as love, sex, life, death. Money usually important.

9 Energy put into many, often wide-ranging, ventures. May include extended self-education and travel.

10 Energy devoted to the achievement of an ambition. Strong driving force to reach a top position.

11 Much energy devoted to exploring and improving social affairs, creative promotions or group interests.

12 Here energy may be limited or used indirectly, may behave like a rebel or a passive pressure cooker.

JUPITER

Symbolism The prophet.
Area of influence Expansion and freedom.
Associated with optimism, growth space, order; Jupiter's place in the chart shows where your opportunities for improvement lie.

Jupiter in the zodiac signs

Aries Likes to improve the self and use opportunities to the fullest extent. May become too egocentric.

Taurus Likes to improve the value of money and the luxury it can buy. Extravagance can lead to dissipation.

Gemini Likes to be the fun-loving ideas person who is original and alert. Can become temperamental.

Cancer Likes to improve relations with a wide public and to share generously. May get too sentimental.

Leo Likes to improve conditions by making the dream a reality for someone. Can be exuberant or arrogant.

Virgo Likes to improve standards by attention to detail. May make mountains out of molehills or become lazy.

Libra Hospitable, likes to improve leisure time and pleasures, especially with a partner. Hopeless alone.

Scorpio Likes to improve life by thinking big and doing the work to match. Shrewd but can be uncompromising.

Sagittarius Likes to take opportunities to make life brighter for others. Always optimistic, may be reckless.

Capricorn Likes to expand through dedication, hard work, economy. Can be too orthodox or a martyr.

Aquarius Inspired to help people whatever their race or religion. Can be revolutionary or unrealistic.

Pisces Likes to improve the lot of the underdog but quietly and unassumingly. Can be too self-sacrificing.

Jupiter in the houses

1 Broad-minded, breezy, optimistic, humourous, you are the executive type but could become self-indulgent.

2 Prosperous, likable, with wide appeal, you are the business type but could be showy or spendthrift.

3 Witty, happy-go-lucky, you are the type to have good relations with relatives, students or the local public.

4 Generous, loyal, outgoing, you are the head-of-the family type. You like to entertain and to be in control.

5 Dramatic, with wide interests, the happy-family type who also gambles – and wins if not too reckless.

6 Cheerful, usually lucky, you are the type for whom something always turns up. You enjoy your work.

7 Often gaining from others, you are the type to have a happy life and to lavish affection on your partner.

8 Resourceful, discerning, you like to manage the affairs of others. A positive attitude to life and sex.

9 Tolerant, faithful, devoted, you are the type to get along with people from other cultures and religions.

10 Self-reliant, trustworthy, proud, ambitious, you are the leader type but could become overbearing.

11 Benevolent with high aspirations, you enjoy many social contacts and devote time to people.

12 Kind, resourceful in trouble, you like to give in secret, perhaps because you doubt yourself.

SATURN
Symbolism The lawgiver.
Area of influence Responsibility.
Associated with truth and learning;
Saturn's position on the chart shows how
and where you compensate against
insecurity.

The influence of Saturn

Traditionally, Saturn is represented as the cold, barren planet that imposes major restrictions on our lives. Modern astrologers believe, however, that Saturn simply shows us our own limitations. It is up to us to learn the lessons that this planet can teach us, and so to balance our needs realistically. Saturn's position can tell us much about our unconscious feelings of insecurity. The house positions show the possible sources of these feelings; the sign positions indicate how particular talents are developed to try and compensate for them.

Saturn in the zodiac signs

Aries Capable of using ingenuity to develop strength of character. May need to learn tact and cooperation.

Taurus Capable of being trustworthy and patient in everyday affairs. May need to reassess values.

Gemini Capable of being adaptable and systematic in scientific pursuits. May need to learn spontaneity.

Cancer Capable of being shrewd, able and loyal to family or firm. May need to control self-pity and show genuine emotions.

Leo Capable of self-assured leadership in almost any field. May have to learn to enjoy life and laugh.

Virgo Capable of being precise and prudent in detailed work. May need to learn what is important.

Libra Capable of being responsible for work requiring good planning and justice. May need to learn tolerance.

Scorpio Capable of using a subtle, strong willpower to achieve success. May need to learn to forgive and forget.

Sagittarius Capable of building a reputation for being morally outspoken. May need to be less self-righteous.

Capricorn Capable of good organisation and a responsible use of power and prestige. May need to relax.

Aquarius Capable of original abstract thought in any organisation. May need to learn to express gratitude.

Pisces Capable of humility and understanding when working with others. May need to keep track of reality.

Saturn in the houses

1 Sense of personal inadequacy may spur you on.

2 Anxiety due to possessions, money or lack of money.

3 Fear of the unknown or of being lonely.

4 Anxiety about age or being a nobody.

5 Anxiety when trying to express yourself fully.

6 A worrier anxious to prove your worth.

7 Difficulties in one-to-one relationships.

8 Sex and love can be sources of anxiety.

9 New ideas or new places may cause anxiety.

10 Irresponsible power urges cause anxiety.

11 Being given or offered affection can cause anxiety.

12 Anxiousness about life can cause isolation.

URANUS
Symbolism The awakener.
Area of influence Change and freedom.
A generation planet associated with
ideas and the unexpected.
House position shows where you
behave out of character.

Uranus in the zodiac signs

Aries, c.1928–1934 Impetuous, self-willed pioneers
taking charge of their lives and altering destiny.

Taurus, c. 1935–1942 Determined, practical builders of
economic reforms but liable to unexpected trouble.

Gemini, c.1942–1949 Brilliant, inventive people with
original ideas for innovative reforms. Often fickle.

Cancer, c.1949–1956 Emotionally restive people
seeking freedom in the home, marriage and for women.

Leo, c.1956–1962 New rhythms, unconventional
outlooks. Determined to change what does not suit them.

Virgo, c.1962–1968 An inquiring, down-to-earth interest
in ecology, health and advanced technology.

Libra, c. 1968–1975 Charming, magnetic people out to
rectify injustices and give meaning to relationships.

Scorpio, c. 1891–1898 and 1975–1981 Intense, daring,
fascinating, decisive people seeking new approaches.

Sagittarius, c. 1898–1904 and 1981–1988 Equable,
optimistic people with progressive, open minds.

Capricorn, c.1905–1912 and 1988–1995 Responsible
and resourceful people determined to reconcile
conflicts.

Aquarius, c. 1912–1919 and 1995–2002 Strong,
inventive, humanitarian people, free thinkers, but
sometimes impractical.

Pisces, c.1919–1927 Imaginative, visionary and often self-sacrificing, sometimes impractical or escapist.

Uranus in the houses

1 Always out of character compared with your peers as you are often ahead of your time. A nonconformist.

2 Value systems are your speciality since you invent your own to match your need for independence.

3 You behave out of character, often with genius. Open-minded, you are unpredictable and inventive.

4 You may like frequent changes of residence and have a changeable home life. You may fear being alone.

5 You may act out of character with regard to established conventions: marriage, children, rules.

6 You are prone to sudden upsets and minor illnesses and need to work in your own way. Often highly strung.

7 You are likely to be unpredictable or to behave in unusual ways in personal relationships or partnerships.

8 You may experience unconventional or unexpected events concerning money or sex; you experiment.

9 Unorthodox and independent, you may enjoy the unexpected while travelling or in legal matters.

10 Altruistic, you are a great fighter but a bad follower. Career and work are where the unusual may happen.

11 You may have strange, nonconformist ideas but are most likely to make unusual friendships.

12 You may have unusual or secret love affairs or unconscious conflicts that may surface unexpectedly.

NEPTUNE
Symbolism The mystic.
Area of influence Imagination and intuition.

A generation planet associated with the spiritual or escapist urge. House position shows idealistic or self-deceptive trends.

Neptune in the zodiac signs

Aries, c. 1861–1874 Radical missionaries with strong egos, pioneering new philosophical ideas.

Taurus, c. 1874–1887 Artistic and experimental with an instinct for business, but sometimes led astray by others.

Gemini, c. 1887–1901 Alert, inquiring, restless people with new ideas on trade, travel and communications.

Cancer, c. 1901–1915 Emotional, patriotic and mystical with strong ties to home and family despite upheavals.

Leo, c.1915–1929 Speculative, romantic, powerful, bringing flair, idealisation and new developments.

Virgo, c. 1929–1943 Humanitarian, divided between reason and emotion. Throws baby out with bathwater.

Libra, c.1943–1956 Compassionate, peace-loving but impractical; 'doing your own thing' causes problems.

Scorpio, c.1956–1970 Investigative and emotional with interest in new approaches both good and bad.

Sagittarius, c.1970–1984 Frankness reveals things previously hidden and brings out new universal ideals.

Capricorn, c. 1984–1998 Conventional, practical and conscientious – a period of applied knowledge.

Aquarius, c.1998–2012 Detached attitudes with a truly philosophical outlook – the start of a peaceful period.

Pisces Neptune was last here in c.1847–1861, a period of new cultural concepts.

Neptune in the houses

1 You may idealise yourself because you do not see yourself clearly. Charismatic with strong imagination.

2 You are idealistic about possessions but may be very impractical about money. An intuitive sense of value.

3 You dream about your idealistic world but may be vague or feel misunderstood. Persuasive and intuitive.

4 You idealise family or home but may be uncertain about your own identity. Artistic and musical.

5 You idealise romance and the people you love but may need lots of romantic affairs. Very creative.

6 You are idealistic about whatever you do but may drift along or have vague illnesses. Poetic, lonely, sensitive.

7 You idealise others in your life but may need to face the realities. Often influenced by or serving others.

8 You idealise the search for truth but may lead yourself or others astray. Charismatic and intuitive.

9 You idealise social and educational reforms but may be impressionable. Tolerant and intellectual.

10 You idealise your public image but may have self-doubts. High aspirations and awareness of motives.

11 You idealise those who are odd or different but may be unreliable. Generous with an accurate intuition.

12 You idealise insight but may deceive yourself or be deceived. Wise and extremely sensitive. A loner.

PLUTO
Symbolism The dark lord.
Area of influence Transformation.
A generation planet associated with that which is hidden. House position shows the complexities you have to resolve alone.

Pluto in the zodiac signs

Aries, c.1823–1851 A desire for reform, power or revenge. Great daring, initiative, imagination.

Taurus, c.1851–1883 The growth of materialism with a great need for wealth, security and permanence.

Gemini, c. 1883–1913 A time of major changes through new inventions. Impetuous, intellectual, critical.

Cancer, c.1913–1938 A period of great upheaval, pride and patriotism. Social awareness and a need for security.

Leo, c. 1938–1957 A period when power was sought and developed. Self-confidence, perversity, business skill.

Virgo, c.1957–1971 A period of intensive technical development. Analytical, inventive, perfecting.

Libra, c. 1971–1983 A period of social changes inspired by a sense of justice. Adaptable, responsible, but fickle.

Scorpio, c.1983–1995 A period predicted as innovative and may be redemptive. Environmental sensitivity.

Sagittarius, c. 1995–? The period predicted to be very reformative with a return to fundamental laws.

Capricorn A predicted period of efficiency, ambition and an emphasis on organisation and management.

Aquarius Predicted as a period of revelation and a love of freedom. Unconventional, revolutionary, ingenious.

Pisces Predicted as the next period of enlightenment in human history, a period of compassion and sensitivity.

Pluto in the houses

1 An urge to resolve the complete expression of the many sides of your strong, creative personality.

2 An urge to turn liabilities into assets and to prevent assets ruining your happiness.

3 An urge to make yourself heard, resolve your shortcomings, and face changes in your life.

4 An urge to identify and resolve the complexities of your origins and to transform yourself.

5 An urge to take risks and resolve your strong erotic, creative and emotional feelings.

6 An urge to resolve your mission in life in your own very individualistic way.

7 An urge to use your dynamic personality to resolve issues of interpersonal circumstances.

8 An urge to investigate and resolve all hidden desires, obsessions or mysteries – your own or other people's.

9 An adventurous urge to resolve a dream by trying absolutely everything life has to offer.

10 An urge courageously to resolve a need to assert yourself and gain identity or acclaim.

11 An urge to resolve your intense desire to reform the world single-handed.

12 An urge to resolve inner fears and frustrations, or to change personal limitations.

ASPECTS

Aspects are the different angular relationships between the planets on a birth chart; they reveal connections between the areas of personality represented by the planets. Aspects may emphasise, challenge or show where adjustments may have to be made between the different parts of the personality in action. They are neither good nor bad; something of everything is needed to make a whole human being. Too much ease can become boring; too much stress can result in bitterness. Depth of character comes from a balance between tension and relaxation.

An understanding of the natural aspects between the signs of the zodiac is the key to interpreting the aspects between planets in those signs. Here we look at the six major aspects and how to locate and interpret them on a chart.

THE SIX MAJOR ASPECTS

These are the six angular relationships that are consistently given importance by astrologers because they describe the relationships between all the elements and qualities of the zodiac signs. Some astrologers also use up to ten minor aspects to emphasise the finer points of the major aspects.

Each angle or aspect has a symbol, a name, an orb and a specific meaning. The orb is the number of degrees of deviation allowed from the exact angle of the aspect.

1 Conjunction Planets in the same sign act in the same way and concentrate their energies.

2 Opposition Conflict between opposite signs produces a potential for self-awareness and perspective.

3 Square Tension between the elemental ways in which

two planets operate offers a challenge.
4 Sextile Planets placed in compatible signs offer
opportunities.
5 Trine A satisfying, easy combination of planets.
6 Inconjunct Planets in signs that have nothing in
common suggest a need to reorganise or reconcile parts
of the self.

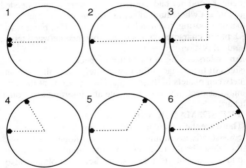

Symbol	Name	Angle	Orb	Meaning
1 ☌	Conjunction	0°	7°	Concentration
2 ☍	Opposition	180°	7°	Perspective
3 ☐	Square	90°	7°	Challenge
4 ✳	Sextile	60°	5°	Opportunity
5 △	Trine	120°	7°	Satisfaction
6 ⅄	Inconjunct*	150°	5°	Reorganisation

*Sometimes known as the quincunx.

THREE OR MORE PLANETS IN THE SAME ASPECT

a The stellium Three or more planets that lie within seven degrees of each other on the chart are called a stellium. Here the emphasis is even greater than a conjunction of two planets; individuality or a special interest are often indicated in this way. Conjunctions of this kind are often found on the splay-shaped charts.

b T-Square When one planet is square to two others in opposition a T-square is formed.

c Grand square Four planets in opposition are square to each other forming the most powerful aspect that can be found on any chart; sometimes this aspect is called a grand cross.

d Grand trine Three planets in trine aspect form a grand trine, an aspect of ease, pleasure and harmony.

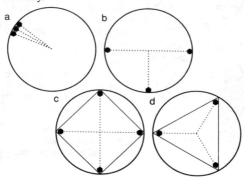

SQUARES AND OPPOSITIONS

These are always aspects between planets in cardinal (**A**), fixed (**B**) or mutable (**C**) signs.

Squares are the building blocks of a chart, indicating decisions and actions to be taken as a result of the challenges presented by life. They may indicate turning points, potential accomplishments or disruptions.

Oppositions can show areas where one polarity can compensate for something lacking in the other. They give perspective and can be areas of cooperation or conflict.

The quality of the aspects shows how decisions are made and action taken: cardinal aspects operate quickly and with the intention of solving the situation; fixed aspects are slow and deliberate and may show an acceptance of the situation; mutable aspects indicate variable actions that are often influenced by other people.

POLARITIES BETWEEN THE SIGNS AND THE HOUSES

The way in which identity is expressed by the different signs of the zodiac is a key to understanding the polarities between signs in opposition. The 'good' and 'bad' polarities that can exist within each identity are shown in the list.

The house positions also have their opposites. Although houses as such are not regarded as being in opposition, the placing of the aspects in houses will show the area of life to which the aspect applies. Reading across the list the identity of the signs can be matched with their natural houses.

It is important to be aware that meanings should never be taken too literally; the art of good astrological interpretation lies in the ability to comprehend the wider, more symbolic meanings of the keywords. For example, investments are not necessarily financial: we may invest energy, time and space.

SIGN	IDENTITY	SIGN	IDENTITY
Aries ♈	I exist Me first	**Cancer** ♋	I feel I brood
Taurus ♉	I have I indulge	**Leo** ♌	I will I pretend
Gemini ♊	I think I scheme	**Virgo** ♍	I study I worry

SIGN	IDENTITY	SIGN	IDENTITY
Libra ♎	I cooperate I procrastinate	**Capricorn** ♑	I use I inhibit
Scorpio ♏	I desire I suspect	**Aquarius** ♒	I know I'm unreliable
Sagittarius ♐	I understand I exaggerate	**Pisces** ♓	I believe I escape

HOUSE	AREAS	HOUSE	AREAS
1	Myself Outlook	**7**	Yourself Partnership
2	What is mine Values	**8**	What is yours Investments
3	Life here and near Awareness	**9**	Life there and far Optimism and learning
4	Private life/source Security	**10**	Public life/image Status
5	What I give Creativity	**11**	What I receive Ideas
6	Physical health Service	**12**	Mental health Secrets

SEXTILES AND TRINES

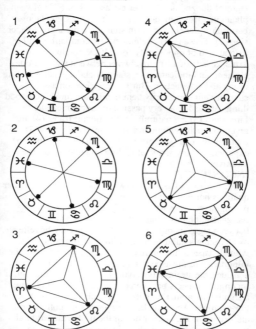

These are always aspects between planets in harmonious signs of the zodiac. Sextiles are aspects of 60° between a planet in a fire sign and a planet in an air sign (1), or between a planet in an earth sign and a planet in a water sign (2). These pairs of elements are compatible and offer a great deal of opportunity for self-expression.

Trine aspects of 120° are always between signs of one element, and indicate ease, stability and a general feeling of joy and satisfaction. But several trines on a chart are not necessarily beneficial – too much of a good thing can lead to a very passive or indolent existence. Fire trines (3) are naturally energetic; air trines (4) are given to much thought and idealism: earth trines (5) are found in the charts of practical realists: water trines (6) experience every shade of feeling and may be quite intuitive.

INCONJUNCTS

These are always aspects between signs that have neither qualities nor elements in common. Consequently they may indicate areas where an adjustment or some reorganisation has to take place. There is a strain between signs inconjunct, and this strain may be relieved by changing a habit or re-thinking a whole policy. As with all aspects, the more exact the angle the greater the importance of the aspect: an exact 150° angle indicates considerable strain between the two planets in the signs. Inconjunct aspects between the signs are easy to locate: a sign is inconjunct with the sign each side of its opposite. For example, Aries can be inconjunct with both Scorpio and Virgo, or with either one of them (A): the cardinal fire sign of Aries has nothing in common with either the fixed water sign of Scorpio or the mutable earth sign of

Virgo. Double aspects of inconjunction are doubly problematic.

CONJUNCTIONS

These aspects occur when planets are within 7° of each other: the planets may be in the same sign or in adjoining signs. Conjunctions concentrate energy, whose focus is determined by the sign and house position of the aspect. Shown on the chart are examples of an exact conjunction and a stellium.

a An exact conjunction of Neptune and the moon at 28° of Virgo. The moon conjunct Neptune is an extremely sensitive and impressionable combination, making it difficult to tell illusion from reality. Virgo, however, ensures discrimination, but will add a strong pull between reason and emotion.

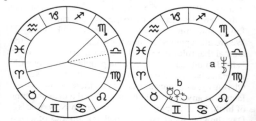

b A stellium of Uranus, Venus and Saturn at 2°, 3° and 9° respectively of Gemini. This indicates a self-willed, original, detached, fickle, sparkling stroke of genius, perhaps the result of a great need for security. Saturn's presence indicates that happiness and duty are seen as synonymous.

Oriental astrology

Just as in the west most people know the name of their
astrological sun sign (Aries, Taurus and so on), so in
the east they know the name of the year of their birth –
the year of the dog, the year of the goat and so on.
It is said that the Buddha invited all the animals to
celebrate the New Year with him, but only 12 came.
As a reward, the Buddha named a year after each of
them. These years still run in the order in which the 12
arrived in his presence, with the rat first and the pig
last.

And so oriental astrology is based on a 12-year cycle.
Each year of the cycle is a lunar year, based on the
phases of the moon. Consequently, each year begins on
a different date according to the western calendar,
falling some time between January 21 and February 21.
We are all supposed to inherit the characteristics of the
animal that rules the year of our birth. And each animal
is held to influence not only the people born in one of
its years, but also the actual nature of the year itself.
Obviously, as in western astrology, there are other
factors in any individual horoscope – the date and time
of birth, for example, with those born on New Year's
Day showing the most marked characteristics of a sign.
But detailed prediction in oriental astrology is
extremely complex: at least two Chinese astrologers
were executed by their Emperors for failing to predict
the future correctly . . .

Lo-king plate

The ancient Chinese consulted a horoscope disc, the lo-king, in order to predict the future. The 12 animals of their zodiac appear around the outside, and details of the stars and planets in the center.

THE ANIMALS AND THEIR YEARS

The 12-year cycle of the animals is shown in the list. (In Vietnam, the year of the rabbit is known as the year of the cat.) A special year of the horse – the year of the fire horse – occurs every 60 years.

1955 GOAT (January 24, 1955 – February 11, 1956)
1956 MONKEY (February 12, 1956 – January 30, 1957)
1957 ROOSTER (January 31, 1957 – February 18, 1958)
1958 DOG (February 19, 1958 – February 7, 1959)
1959 PIG (February 8, 1959 – January 27, 1960)
1960 RAT (January 28, 1960 – February 15, 1961)
1961 BUFFALO (February 16, 1961– February 4, 1962)

1962 TIGER (February 5, 1962 - January 25, 1963)
1963 RABBIT (January 26, 1963 – February 13, 1964)
1964 DRAGON (February 14, 1964 – February 2, 1965)
1965 SNAKE (February 3, 1965 – January 21, 1966)
1966 FIRE HORSE (January 22, 1966 – February 8, 1967)
1967 GOAT (February 9, 1967 – January 29, 1968)
1968 MONKEY (January 30, 1968 – February 16, 1969)
1969 ROOSTER (February 17, 1969 – February 5, 1970)
1970 DOG (February 6, 1970 – January 26, 1971)
1971 PIG (January 27, 1971 – February 18, 1972)
1972 RAT (February 19, 1972 – February 2, 1973)
1973 BUFFALO (February 3, 1973 – January 23, 1974)
1974 TIGER (January 24, 1974 – February 10, 1975)
1975 RABBIT (February 11, 1975 – January 30, 1976)
1976 DRAGON (January 31, 1976 – February 17, 1977)
1977 SNAKE (February 18, 1977 – February 7, 1978)
1978 HORSE (February 8, 1978 – January 27, 1979)
1979 GOAT (January 28, 1979 – February 15, 1980)
1980 MONKEY (February 16, 1980 – February 4, 1981)
1981 ROOSTER (February 5, 1981 – January 24, 1982)
1982 DOG (January 25, 1982 – February 12, 1983)
1983 PIG (February 13, 1983 – February 1, 1984)
1984 RAT (February 2, 1984 – February 19, 1985)
1985 BUFFALO (February 20, 1985 – February 8, 1986)
1986 TIGER (February 9, 1986 – January 28, 1987)
1987 RABBIT (January 29, 1987 – February 16, 1988)
1988 DRAGON (February 17, 1988 – February 5, 1989)
1989 SNAKE (February 6, 1989 – January 26, 1990)
1990 HORSE (January 27, 1990 – February 14, 1991)
1991 GOAT (February 15, 1991 –   )

THE INFLUENCE OF THE YEARS

1 In the year of the rat

Save up for the future, read the good books that will be published and expect political surprises. A good year for rats, buffalo, dragons, monkeys and pigs; a bad year for tigers, rabbits, horses, goats and roosters; an indifferent year for snakes and dogs.

2 In the year of the buffalo

Look after your garden, enjoy the good harvest and take care not to be overworked. A good year for buffalo, horses, monkeys and roosters; a bad year for tigers, snakes, goats and dogs; an indifferent year for rats, rabbits, dragons and pigs.

3 In the year of the tiger

Try to find a little peace and quiet, but expect major changes in your life, and political upheavals (anything from snap elections to revolutions). A good year for tigers, dragons, horses and dogs; a bad year for buffalo, rats, roosters and goats; an indifferent year for rabbits, snakes, pigs and monkeys.

4 In the year of the rabbit
Take full advantage of a quiet
year that allows you to rest, take
holidays and enjoy the company
of friends. A good year for
rabbits, dragons, snakes, horses,
goats and monkeys; a bad year
for rats; an indifferent year for
buffalo, tigers, roosters, dogs and
pigs.

5 In the year of the dragon
Be ambitious and enterprising,
and enjoy an exciting, successful
and exhausting year. A year that
can set the world on fire –
literally as well as figuratively. A
good year for rats, tigers,
dragons, monkeys and roosters; a
bad year for dogs; an indifferent
year for buffalo, rabbits, snakes,
pigs, horses and goats.

6 In the year of the snake
Be a lotus-eater, and enjoy a lazy,
hedonistic year, as all your
problems will appear to have
been solved. A good year for
rabbits, dragons, snakes, goats,
monkeys and dogs; a bad year for
rats, buffalo and tigers; an
indifferent year for roosters,
horses and pigs.

7 In the year of the horse

Get involved, but be tactful with the ruffled tempers around you; this irritability increases in the year of the fire horse. A good year for buffalo, dragons, goats and roosters; a bad year for horses (especially the year of the fire horse), rats, snakes and pigs; an indifferent year for tigers, rabbits, monkeys and dogs.

8 In the year of the goat

Be yourself, and try to find time for a little self-indulgence as you and the world muddle through a series of major and minor crises. A good year for goats, monkeys and pigs; a bad year for buffalo, tigers, roosters and dogs; an indifferent year for rats, rabbits, dragons, snakes and horses.

9 In the year of the monkey

Take some risks, launch some new ideas and expect the unexpected. As no-one is thinking before they act, rebellions, revolutions and insurrections are all possible. A good year for rats, tigers, horses, goats, dogs, pigs, monkeys and roosters; a bad year for buffalo; an indifferent year for rabbits, dragons and snakes.

10 In the year of the rooster

Keep scratching around to make a living as unemployment rises, and watch your behaviour while the forces of law and order are in full cry. A good year for rats, dragons, horses, roosters and pigs; a bad year for tigers, rabbits and snakes; an indifferent year for buffalo, goats, dogs and monkeys.

11 In the year of the dog

Although you feel very defensive, don't be too pessimistic as there is a great deal of idealism and generosity around. A good year for rats, dragons, dogs and pigs; a bad year for buffalo, snakes, goats and roosters; an indifferent year for tigers, rabbits, horses and monkeys.

12 In the year of the pig

Enjoy yourself, as there is enough of everything for everyone, and plenty to spare. Especially good for intellectuals and anyone setting out to make money. A good year for rats, tigers, rabbits, dragons, horses, monkeys and pigs; a bad year for no-one; an indifferent year for buffalo, snakes, goats, roosters and dogs.

CHARACTERISTICS

Rat

A charming but aggressive opportunist. Clever, elegant, light-hearted and sentimental. A gossip who needs company, a grumbler who can be a constructive critic. A bargain-hunter who hoards for the future and who is frightened of failure. Compatible with the dragon, buffalo and monkey; incompatible with the rabbit and horse.

Tiger

A magnetic, respected leader whose stubbornness can lead to trouble. A rash, rebellious hothead who is also sensitive, introspective and intensely emotional. Critical, quarrelsome, passionate, protective, lacking trust in others and sometimes very indecisive. Capable of both petty meanness and grand, generous gestures. Compatible with the horse, dragon or dog; incompatible with the snake, monkey, buffalo and rabbit.

Dragon

A gifted, generous, tactless, tenacious, demanding perfectionist who does everything (including the wrong things) very thoroughly. Honest, proud, enthusiastic, healthy and energetic, an idealist who is always successful. A lover of show and spectacle whose apparent air of superiority hides a deep-down discontent.

Compatible with the rat, snake, rooster and monkey; incompatible with the dog and buffalo.

Buffalo

A velvet hand in an iron glove – an affectionate, introspective idealist hiding behind a down-to-earth, authoritarian exterior. Placid and patient, but when roused the iron glove becomes a dangerous fist. A clever, original and methodical mind hiding behind a conventional facade. A trustworthy, possessive conservative who can become prosperous only through hard work.

Compatible with the rooster, rat and snake; incompatible with the monkey, goat and tiger.

Rabbit

A warm, affectionate friend
who is clever, contented and
peace-loving. A bit of a show-
off who enjoys company and
entertains with traditional and
generous hospitality.
Sympathetic and sentimental,
proud and condescending,
cautious and industrious,
apparently mysterious but
sometimes superficial.
Compatible with the goat, dog
and pig; incompatible with the
rat, tiger and rooster.

Snake

An elegant, attractive, self-
critical philosopher who can be
a good-natured snob. An
amusing, sentimental, romantic
flirt who can be decisive and
determined. Wise and intuitive,
lazy and cautious, slow to anger
but a bad loser when crossed.
Possessive, lucky with money
and inclined to help in kind
rather than in cash. A tendency
to exaggeration and ostentation.
Compatible with the rooster,
buffalo, dragon and dog;
incompatible with the tiger and
pig.

Horse

A popular extrovert who can
succeed at almost anything when
at the center of attention. Quick-
witted and cunning, attractive and
healthy, loving crowds and
flattery – a born politician. An
impatient, intemperate egotist
who lacks self-confidence, will
never listen to advice and who
would give up everything for
love. A fire horse carries these
tendencies to extremes, and can
burn out from excess.

Compatible with the goat, dog,
tiger and rooster; incompatible
with the rat, monkey, buffalo
and pig.

Monkey

An intelligent, amusing,
exuberant egotist, apparently
friendly but in fact contemptuous.
A vain, unscrupulous opportunist,
inventive and curious, with a
good memory. Independent,
ambitious, successful and good
with money. Enthusiastic initially
but easily bored, preferring
infatuation to love.

Compatible with the dragon, rat
and goat; incompatible with the
tiger, horse and pig.

Dog

A shy, stubborn, introverted worrier, a cynical pessimist who becomes engrossed in details, ignoring the larger picture. A loyal, honest, reliable, courageous idealist with a strong sense of justice. Intelligent but inarticulate, anti-social but a good listener, discreet, dependable and inspiring confidence. A hard worker, generous, but not good with money. Compatible with the horse, tiger and rabbit; incompatible with the dragon and goat.

Goat

A graceful, creative hedonist, happiest when supported by others who will bear all responsibility. A weak-willed, duplicitous worrier who craves security, and is often the helpless center of attention. Lacks any sense of time, any self-control and any respect for anyone else's property. Tends to assume that the grass must always be greener on the other side of every fence, and so is frequently discontented. Compatible with the horse, pig, rabbit and monkey; incompatible with the buffalo and dog.

Rooster

A popular, creative daydreamer
who likes people but needs
occasional solitude, who dislikes
routine but works well under
pressure. A frank advice-giver,
leading a very up-and-down life,
who loves and needs to be praised.
Extravagant and self-satisfied, a
boaster who undertakes too much
but sometimes succeeds beyond
all expectations.
Compatible with the buffalo,
snake, horse, dragon, dog and rat;
incompatible with the rabbit and
other roosters.

Pig

A transparently honest and
trusting pacifist, innocent, gullible
and easily taken advantage of.
Gallant and courteous, stubborn,
scrupulous, and uncompromising,
a loyal friend. Neither competitive
nor good with money, but
occasionally becoming rich. A sad
and sensitive sensualist, an
intellectual who reads
indiscriminately.
Compatible with the rabbit and
dragon; incompatible with the
goat and snake.